THE KABBALAH MONOGRAPHS

THE WORK OF BRIAH

[THE SET OF THE WORLD]

THE MASTER OF HIDDENNESS

THE CONFIGURATIONS

Reviews and endorsements for Jason Shulman's work

About The Instruction Manual for Receiving God:

"A Dharma teacher and Kabbalist, Jason Shulman has succeeded in creating a down-to-earth guide which makes the quest to find God into a realizable possibility."

> — Deepak Chopra, M.D., author of *Life After Death: The Burden of Proof*

"Beautiful lessons and brilliant insights on the divine nature of humanity and how we connect with God and ourselves. Enlightening and inspirational."

> — Stephen R. Covey, author, *The 7 Habits of Highly Effective People* and *The 8th Habit: From Effectiveness to Greatness*

"*The Instruction Manual for Receiving God* contains exactly the type of common sense wisdom required for a person to live a good old-fashioned grounded life in a society that encourages us to do things faster while multi-tasking. This book is a magnificent breath of tranquil air."

> — Caroline Myss, author of *Anatomy of the Spirit* and *Sacred Contracts*

"Jason Shulman offers us a profoundly simple guide to the obviousness of awakening to our deepest Self. Lucid, contemporary, and most of all kind, this is a beautiful book which goes to the very heart of the human condition, by encouraging us to embrace both the impersonal oneness of all things and the richness of the personal life."

> — Timothy Freke, author of *Lucid Living*

A beautiful book that brings the Western spiritual tradition into our modern world. It's deep, thoughtful, exciting, and we can use it to find out how we live when we are fully human."

— John Tarrant, author of *Bring Me the Rhinoceros*

About Kabbalistic Healing: A Path to an Awakened Soul:

"Jason Shulman is a true adept of the inner teachings. He offers a very sophisticated and dynamic account of what happens between the Kabbalah and the great, luminous transparency. To engage with Jason Shulman's mind is to enter into the reality where true healing can occur."

— Rabbi Zalman Schachter-Shalomi, Founder of the Jewish Renewal Movement

"This lucid book of deep healing is a brilliant contribution to the spiritual literature bridging Eastern and Western thought. Shulman's bigger view unifies seeking and being-there, path and goal, transcendence and immanence, with the joy of a true master."

— Lama Surya Das, founder of the Dzogchen Center and author of *Awakening the Buddha Within*

"Jason Shulman brilliantly integrates a deep psychological component with a profound understanding of the non-dual, absolute unity of the Divine Nature in a way that raises the reader's soul to the highest potential of awareness. While traditional teachings tend to demean the ego-self, Shulman shows us the importance of our gift of self-awareness and how to come to peace with ourselves. Thus he leads readers to evoke a healing from our sense of fractured separation into a wholeness of being that has compassion for who we are and what we are. This is a must-read for anyone who wishes to learn the essence of kabbalistic teachings in the hands of a master of spiritual and psychological development."

— Rabbi David A. Cooper, author of *God Is a Verb*

"Here is once and future wisdom as we meet the Jewish mystical tradition in its revelatory mapping of the nature of reality. Here too are practices that bring the reader closer to the nondual state of consciousness and awareness of the integral relationship between all things. Taken seriously, this profound work can only charge the spirit as it illumines the mind and heart."

— Jean Houston, PH.D., author of *Jump Time: Shaping Your Future in a World of Radical Change*

"Kabbalistic Healing is a great book about discovering wisdom within each of us. At a time when everyone in contemporary society is experiencing an information glut, what's missing is a deeper understanding of life. Jason Shulman provides the reader with wisdom and insight for life's journey."

— Stephan Rechtschaffen, cofounder of the Omega Institute for Holistic Studies, and creator and director of Blue Spirit Costa Rica.

"Jason Shulman is a sincere, authentic practitioner of Kabbalah. The fruit of much inner work, the masterful teachings in this book resonate and come alive because he has truly experienced this wisdom from deep inside."

— Rabbi Tirzah Firestone, author of *The Receiving: Reclaiming Jewish Women's Wisdom* and *With Roots in Heaven*

Other works by Jason Shulman

The Nondual Shaman: A Contemporary Shamanistic
Path & Thoroughgoing Training for Awakening the Self

Ecstatic Speech: Expressions of True Nonduality

The MAGI Process: A Nondual Method for Personal
Awakening and the Resolution of Conflict

What does reward bring you but to bind you
to Heaven like a slave? (Poetry)

The Instruction Manual for Receiving God

Kabbalistic Healing: A Path to an Awakened Soul

THE KABBALAH MONOGRAPHS

THE WORK OF BRIAH

[THE SET OF THE WORLD]

THE MASTER OF HIDDENNESS

THE CONFIGURATIONS

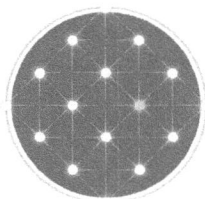

THE FOUNDATION
FOR NONDUALITY
Jason Shulman Library

The Foundation for Nonduality
Oldwick, New Jersey 08833

Series Editor: Nancy Yielding
Series Managing Editor: Kimberly Burnham
Editorial Counselor: Shelah Stein
Cover and interior design: Tom Schneider
MS Word mise-en-scéne: Jeff Casper

The Kabbalah Monographs
Copyright © 2018 by Jason Shulman.

Cover Illustration: Joan Miró

FACSIMILE EDITION 2018

ISBN: 978-0-9972201-2-4

10 9 8 7 6 5 4 3 2 1

Contents

Introduction

In 1996 I created the first brochure that described a school I had decided to found called *A Society of Souls*. After it was printed, I sent copies to people I knew, and I sent one to a rabbi I had read an article about, Reb Zalman Schachter-Shalomi, may everyone who remembers him be blessed by that memory. I knew practically nothing about Reb Zalman, but a voice spoke to me and said *"Send it to him."* So I did.

A few weeks later I got a call: "Jason, this is Reb Zalman. I got your brochure. When I got it I said to myself *Oy! Jason Shulman, a Kabbalist!* But then I read what you had written in the brochure and I knew that the *bubbehs* and *zaydes* spoke to you." The grandmothers and grandfathers. Yes, they have always spoken to me but I didn't dare admit that until Reb Zalman offered me the opportunity to confess my connections aloud. So great was his kindness.

A second Reb Zalman story: Several years later I called Reb Zalman from my home in New Jersey and said, *"I want to discuss something with you. Can I come out and have lunch?"* Zalman lived in Boulder, Colorado. He said, *"Can't we do it on the phone?"* "No," I said. So I flew out to Colorado expecting to have a few hours of his time. We ended up spending two days together talking. After one part of the conversation, where I was concentrating on my connection to what I thought was Absolute Reality in my Advaitic studies, he said to me *"I'm interested in the God of this planet. The God of this time."*

It took me many years to understand that utterance in my bones and, most importantly, in my heart. My life had to get smaller first, until it was the proper-sized vessel that could accept the infinite in a palm-sized heart. I had to climb all the way to some real or imagined pinnacle and then descend again to the place Reb Zalman had pointed out, the place he lived. This valley. This earth. This here and now, with its colors of fall, its bone-white winters and light green springs and sometimes heavy and wet summers. This place of storms and gratitude.

These monographs, which in a sense trace my thinking about Kabbalah over a period of some twenty-five years, are all meant to help us make this planet our home, to make this fleeting time allotted to us useful and beautiful, to make the most vaunted spiritual discourse point us in the direction of what is really important: the love of everything we were born into. They are meant—for those of us who find an earthy fragrance in words about ideas—to encourage all of us to be strong and flexible, to never give up, in the words of another sage, Reb Nachman of Breslov, and to concentrate on being the love we so long to receive.

This is essentially a facsimile edition, which collects three of the monographs and adds a new one on the *Partzufim,* written in 2017. May they inch us toward understanding our true nature.

Jason Shulman
Oldwick, New Jersey

The Work of Briah

Jason Shulman

אדם קדמון שני

עתיק יומין

אנפין

אבא

H uman beings have an odd problem: Our brains are "whole-making machines"; that is, our brains create an undivided totality from pieces of things, and then orient us within that newly perceived pattern. Sometimes this process uncovers a deep structure within reality. But on a deeper level, the level where we want a true connection with the world, this process is only the herald of neuroses, and hence distances us from the very thing we want.

By and large, this pattern-making and wholeness-making machinery exists because there is a Wholeness that is not ego-based or ego-controlled, which our everyday consciousness has learned to deny, and so, in a kind of desperation for Completeness, this ego-consciousness seeks to make things into Wholenesses that are really simulacra of the Real Thing.

In life we are confronted with a continuum of human themes ranging from the simple actions of the world such as *this goes here, do that*, and so on, to the unspoken but omnipresent *relationships* which are on a much more essential level, and which mold the entire conduct of our lives because they speak to our essence as human beings.

I call these essential relational conditions *root-relationships* and *root-metaphors,* depending upon the kabbalistic universe we are describing them from.

When we are dealing with "root-relationships," such as "mother," "father," and so on, and "root-metaphors" like "open-ness," "closed-ness," and so on, the brain, which is not seeing the real Wholeness, will seek to *invent Wholeness from the pieces available to it from its limited perspective and enlarge those pieces into a pretend Whole.*

To restate:

> We have Wholeness in us. In fact, we are made of Wholeness.

> It has become buried, but an echo remains.

> When confronted by True Wholeness in the form of root-relationships (which happens automatically in the course of life), we take the part-object we know from our history (which is not the *root-metaphor* or *root-relationship*) and make it into something more than a generalization: We attach it to the echo of the True Wholeness within us, which our being continually looks to and for, and tries to create and describe and make a *pseudo-Wholeness.*

(This process is akin to the Jungian concepts of anima and animus: Projecting our anima onto the other, and seeing them as a wholeness is the beginning to no end of trouble.)

These pseudo-Wholes have great staying power, which is to say they are intractable to change because they have become attached to the true root-metaphors/relationship.

The brain ignores the missing essential core, fills in the missing pieces, and so these images remain powerfully present, but not Real.

Then our understanding of the actual root-metaphors and root-relationships become "poisoned" as it were, as their true essences are supplanted by the historical or projected images.

So the process of healing is one of unification in that we must first begin to see how we have made *part-objects* into pseudo-wholes. In other words, we have to go *backwards* and return these *so-called* root-metaphors/relationships into the part-objects they always were. We have to unmask their "wholeness" and see them for what they are: simply pieces.

When we actually see and know that these so-called wholes are really pieces, the generalization loses its power to hurt us and falls back to what it really is: a piece that does not entangle us in a failed history.

When something is rescued from its identity as a pseudo-whole and seen clearly as a part-object, the formally poisoned *foreground* recedes into a historically poisoned *background*, which does not impinge upon present consciousness in the same way and leaves a feeling of spaciousness, openness, and flowingness.

This strengthens the ego in the right way, and relationship with the Whole can occur. It is like adding an ingredient to colored water, which precipitates out the chemical that colored the water. This colored chemical falls to the bottom of the glass, and leaves restored, clear water.

To step out of the quandary of mistaking the parts for the Whole requires great effort; namely, to first identify the parts (as opposed to the Whole); that is, to identify that they *are indeed* parts and not the Whole.

This means that people need to follow the dissatisfactions of their lives and see that they stem from an image of Reality that has been conditioned by history (that is, past experience) and has been generalized and superimposed over a root-metaphor/relationship.

In this way, psychically detrimental experiences with a particular mother invades the very concept of Mother, thereby injuring the entire chain of being attached to this root-metaphor/relationship. This historical clarification is the work of therapy.

Root-metaphors and root-relationships, as out-picturings of the informational matrix which shapes our lives, are at the interface between our *personal* and *transcendental* selves, and are the funnels through which Reality unfolds from the cosmic to the particular.

Said another way: these root-metaphors/relationships govern not only human, personal life, but the materially external (and seemingly objective) world, and the psychically transcendental (and seemingly subjective) world as well.

The clarification of the root-metaphors/relationships cannot happen until part-objects are refined out of the psyche. Then the root-concepts, instead of being an expression of a false-whole and therefore a limitation, can be the vehicle through which our human life is fully explored.

It is through our relationships with others that the distortion in our root-metaphors/relationships comes into play.

To maintain the illusion that a psychic and emotional interaction we have with someone is resonant with the Whole of that root-relationship, or put another way, that some *quality* of a person—physical, emotional, or psychic—is the *entire* person, requires that a person *leave Reality* to some extent and exist in a mental construct that appears to be Real, but is not.

This mental construct seems to have "Seeing the Wholeness" as its mission, but in actuality it has neither the capacity, nor the inclination to really do this. This part of us that wishes to See and Relate but will not and cannot we can call the ego.

The ego is always interested in relationship—as is the Real Self—but *only a type of relationship, one in which the ego is at the center, or kept safe from Life, and so on. In other words, the ego is not interested in <u>equal</u> relationships, but only ones where there is a basic <u>inequality</u> between it and the other.*

The ego gets its self-definition from the battle of inequality.

This fantasy that we are really in relationship with the Whole requires a constant effort on the part of the perceiver which reduces the amount of energy left to see Reality as it is. Instead a private story substitutes for the Whole.

Stepping out into Reality requires a particular type of consciousness, or rather a series of new attitudes.

First is the historical study and understanding of the origins of neurosis: This helps the person begin to separate *their own self and that of the other person.* In Kabbalah we might call this the first stage of work in the Universe of Yetzirah.

However, even this approach will not dissolve the part-object completely.

To do that, the person must proceed to the next stage. This next stage requires a particular way of working with energy, which I will call "alchemical." This means: *allowing the tangled energy of the illusion to remain completely vivid without engaging it.* We might kabbalistically call this the work of the first stage of Briah.

In Kabbalah, the movement from one universe to the next is the movement toward the Whole Truth, as opposed to the comparative truth; toward Intelligence of the Heart, from ego-based perception, which is *always the perception of the part taken for the whole.*

In the lowest universe, Asiyah, almost all of Reality is seen only in part: The ego, with its own mission and relationship to history is the ruler here, and Oneness only "leaks" through as experiences which the ego cannot understand or handle, namely great joy or bliss, and great pain or suffering.

The true investigation of this phenomenon takes place in Yetzirah, the psychological universe I mentioned above, to which the suffering individual is propelled as a place of Refuge. Suffering pushes us to territories we might have otherwise demurred to go. Suffering pushes us to ask "why," and "why" pushes us to the psychological realms.

It is here in Yetzirah that some of the underlying dynamics of psychological history are exposed to wisdom, and the parts start being sorted out from the Whole.

This process inevitably leads to many deep moments of emptiness, which the Torah calls *tohu v-bohu*— *formless and void.* This *creative* state of emptiness is the *bardo* through which we are reborn into a new state of energy and being.

The next universe, Briah, is attained or attuned to through the alchemical work, which adds deeply integrative, dynamically moving, karma-shattering consciousness to the yetziratic, psychological interactions.

It is in this place that things are seen "as they are" for the first time, and where part-objects disappear, and the ego's grand scheme of controlling the entire universe is thwarted, in the name of Truth.

In meditation we finally see that what we term "the self" is actually the ego's condensation or constriction of Reality as it is, and as such is yet still another thought, albeit one deep in the psyche, and one which stands very close to the Real Self.

While most thoughts are about *things*, the thought of the ego is the thought of the Self. The ego always seeks to find Who It Is who is relating to the world. The ego perpetually looks outward, seeking relationship, *but only to define itself.* Therefore the ego is in an always-losing battle, never able to look at itself, but only for its reflection in the Eyes of the World.

The Ego Self, because it is so close to the action of the Real Self, is like a penultimate root-metaphor, and therefore has a lot of power to maintain Reality in a certain (egoic) condition and thus set its world around it according to its own array, or in its own part-image.

Specific emotions, which many traditions have identified as "core-sins" are the exclusive property of the ego-self, and are maintained by its powerful life force. These "sins," such as greed, anger, and dullness (depending upon which canon you chose) invade the egoic world in the same way unconscious part-objects invade the psyche of the child. They are—in a way— root-metaphors of darkness, or of disassociated Light. These qualities organize reality around the existence of the ego-self: They have no real existence in terms of the Real Self; that is, they have no existence of their own, but exist only in the belief that there is an egoic self that must be maintained at all costs.

Briatic work with the ego means seeing this vividly, clearly, with great openness and power, and not engaging, escaping, or changing this condition willfully, which is to say, as yet another egoic strategy and drama. It means having come to a place where the ego is healthy enough, where there have been enough temporary experiences of the ego giving up its vaunted place so that the Real Self shines through and gives the individual another place to stand instead of the ego. From this new perspective, the ego can begin to be seen as another fundamental thought of the dreaming self, and the ego's insistence that the world is the way it says it is, that *its* version of the root-relationships and metaphors is the correct one, is seen as the historical inaccuracy that it is.

Alchemy is not the transmutation of one substance into another, as we were led to believe from the old tales of turning lead into gold. True alchemy is the transmutation of something into itself, into its essence, and therefore is the true work of the level of Briah, a universal level which is not concerned with the things as *symbols* but *things-as-themselves*.

When we have done enough work on an historical level so that our egos are healthy enough to engage the primal and unadorned energies of life, it becomes possible to do this alchemical work of vividness by virtue of having a "container" strong and flexible enough to allow "something" to return to "Nothing."

This means that when a feeling or thought is fully engaged and held, with no seduction, aversion, hope, fear, or continued searching, it returns the portion of Reality it has screened off from the Whole *to* the Whole, and the Whole becomes visible; it is Seen.

Put another way, when these difficult energies are held without thought of escape, they become coherent instead of dissonant, and thereby can resonate with the All, sounding the sound of Wholeness. Thus, what was a problem becomes its own solution, and the difficulty—while paradoxically remaining intact—also becomes "Nothing," that is: without concepts, without hindrance. It disappears as an obstacle to being with God.

Root-metaphors and relationships are expressions of, and spring from, this unhindered relationship. They rarely exist 'in vivo' because they have become overlaid with historical confusion; they have become part-objects that have been grafted onto the true experiences, and in most cases, confused with and taken for them.

Everyday language—we might call this the language of Asiyah—is symbolic: one thing *stands* for another. The distance between the two things is very great. So "water" *stands symbolically* for the liquid we drink, but the association of this word with this thing is tenuous at best.

As we move from Asiyah to Yetzirah, language and its power change. The words we use now try to capture the feeling, tone, texture, and essence of what we are talking about in some way. And while language is not yet at its essential bedrock, much more essence is transmitted, and the distance between the word(s) and the thing(s) is smaller.

To wit: Thomas Traherne describing *The Odor of Heaven:*

> *These hands are jewels to the eye,*
> *Like wine, or oil, or honey, to the taste:*
> *These feet which here I wear beneath the sky*
> *Are us'd, yet never waste.*
> *My members all do yield a sweet perfume;*
> *They minister delight, yet not consume.*

One can sense that the thing Traherne is talking about and the words he uses form a closer identity than mere description.

By the time we descend to the level of Briah, we are working with words that are themselves the things we are talking about. This can be understood only by the experience in the moment of using them and the return of "something" to "Nothing" that occurs when we inhabit these words.

Someone can be "happy," a word that has hundreds of volumes between it and what we might be happy about. Another word: "closeness"—more Briatic in the fundamental condition it describes—shows us that this *essential quality* can be experienced kinesthetically and spiritually, and with little or no separation between it and its referent, the essential, universal quality of "being near each other."

The transmutation of language from the symbolic words of Asiyah, through the emotional/psychological ones of Yetzirah to the essential ones of Briah, has its endpoint in the highest level of Briah, where it touches Atzilut, the Place where all words end.

In the Briatic place, we find the final words, the words that are so essential that they are the home for the very essence of the potent forces that created us and the world. These root-metaphors we call the Names of God.

And while the True Name is Unutterable, cannot be contained, limited, explained, or even thought about, Names that exist at levels somewhat more distant from the Absolute *can* be spoken and do transform the one who Speaks.

These are Creative Words, which—while they can be uttered by anyone—when spoken with fuller understanding, embody within them in a non-symbolic way, the Creative Moment. And while it is impossible for human beings to inhabit these Names completely, the more we do, the closer we come to the Divine Milieu.

Because these Names are at the bottom of our lives, visibly existent in Briah, and more invisibly in Yetzirah and Asiyah, we might say that the essence of Eternity is available to all of us, no matter which state of consciousness we happen to be in at the moment, from turmoil to exultation. And that even if we mistake a Name for a magical formula, thereby making it into an idol, the Essential Quality of the Name is so without concepts, that its own Essence is unaffected by our confusion, and is therefore free to guide us, give to us, and shepherd us back to the world of Light.

This combination of the historical work of therapy and the alchemical work of transmutation is essential for returning the part-objects of our soul to the Wholeness they obscure and from which they really come.

Knowing the origins of pain and confusion, feeling this pain and finally, accepting it and letting it be vivid within us, returns to us our essential Wholeness and lets us live the Divine Life we come to know as Human.

[The Set of the World]

Jason Shulman

רְפָאֵנוּ יְיָ וְנֵרָפֵא, הוֹשִׁיעֵנוּ וְנִוָּשֵׁעָה כִּי תְהִלָּתֵנוּ אָתָּה....

Heal us, O Lord, and we will be healed; save us and we will be saved; for You are our praise.

רְפָאֵנוּ יְיָ וְנֵרָפֵא, הוֹשִׁיעֵנוּ וְנִוָּשֵׁעָה כִּי תְהִלָּתֵנוּ אָתָּה....

Heal us, O Lord, and we will be healed; save us and we will be saved; for You are our praise.

PART ONE

Everyone sits in the prison of his own
ideas; he must burst it open, and that in
his youth, and so try to test his ideas on
reality. But in a couple of centuries there
comes another, perhaps, who refutes him.
It is true that this will not happen to the
artist in his uniqueness. It is all within the
nature of research and it is not at all sad.
— *Albert Einstein*

This paper is about Wholeness and how it got to be that way. It describes how our consciousness moves from one level of Wholeness to the next and how Wholeness itself becomes a limitation that leads to suffering and, ultimately, to the understanding of yet a Greater Thing. It also describes how this very movement from Wholeness to Emptiness and back again both creates and is part of the general pulsatory movement of our Universe. It ultimately describes the futility of the ego's search for a resting place devoid of change and the world that awaits us as we let go of fear.

To begin:

In order to go to a deeper level of awareness, the previous level has to be completely Unified.

Stated another way: Deeper levels of truth become visible only as the current level of understanding or the physical, emotional, or spiritual system in question becomes more coherent and resonant. Until that point is reached, we are locked into a small world view with limited perspective.

As an example: A musical string of a certain length, when bowed or struck in the open position makes a tone which is fundamental to that string. Fretting or stopping the string at *different points along the string* creates tones which are based on that open, fundamental tone. However, until we stop "closing the string off," we cannot hear the basic condition of the string in its open state: Since an "A" can be made on many strings of different lengths, until we sound the string in its open position, we do not know the original ground with which we are working.

In areas other than music, the consequences of not knowing the Open State are somewhat more complicated: On a physical, psychological, or spiritual level, when a system or level of awareness is not "working correctly"; that is, when we are enmeshed in either a misconception, a neurosis, or spiritual blindness, when the system or level of awareness is not Coherent or Whole (in its Fundamental state), it can be said to be *turbulent*.

This turbulence then creates *artifacts* in the system.

These artifacts appear to be real and essential creations. The underlying turbulence supplies the energy needed to maintain the existence of these artifacts.

The artifacts then gain a form of limited self-consciousness, become self-organizing and have the appearance of continuously existing.

In this way they are mistaken for Reality. *Systems that reach a coherent state have no turbulence: A Coherent system will exhibit the least amount of energy necessary to maintain its integrity. While artifacts need a lot of energy to remain in existence, Coherent systems show a maximally economical use of energy to maintain structure, freeing up other resources for creativity. In this way, energy is freed up for more Creation instead of for making more confusion or additional obscuring artifacts.*

Psychologically speaking, as awareness of each new level of coherence or resonance is achieved, these artifacts seem to disappear or become *transparent,* and new levels, formerly hidden within that system, come into view. The system becomes economical, with a minimum level of energy expended to keep structures stable.

One example of this movement from turbulence to Coherence is the *diagnostic process* in Integrated Kabbalistic Healing.

In the diagnostic process, we "ride the wave of transference." This means that we make an effort to be present and to keep an open awareness so that we can both participate in and watch the transferential energy that is part of any human encounter. By not defending against either the transference or the imperfection of the interaction, but by being exquisitely aware of and compassionate toward them, we are free to truly see what is going on and to dip below the words to the heart of what is being communicated.

In a sense, the content of the transference becomes *transparent*, and the underlying information is retrieved. We see the artifact (the transference) for what it is (an expression of an incoherent or not-Present state of the speaker), and by *riding the wave*, we allow these artifacts to disappear, not by cutting them out, but by letting their edges soften, so that the temporary content of the moment is replaced by the deeper meaning. This allows us to go the heart of the matter. This is why the diagnostic process is a healing in and of itself.

In kabbalistic terms, this commonly seen process is reflected in our understanding of the Four Universes. If the universe of Asiyah is seen as the *only* real universe, then instead of being seen as an expression of a great wholeness, Asiyah becomes an artifact that obscures the vision of the next deepest universe, Yetzirah. And if Yetzirah is seen as the final paradigm, then that too becomes an artifact created by the turbulence of the small vision and obscures the next deepest level. And so on. The process is one of *fixating* on a single vision of Reality, "taming" it and making it a kind of domestic pet, to be prized and kept in the house, ensconced in some quiet corner. The Four Universes are not separate states, however; and as Coherence comes to each level, that level does not disappear, but becomes *transparent* and allows us to see, within that formerly Cimmerian state, the next level of clarity. Plainly said: In the diagnostic process we allow ourselves to sink from one universe to the next.

In psychological terms, the ego is the artifact created by the turbulence caused by avoiding suffering. The ego is troublesome only when it is seen as the only reality. When it becomes more Coherent or Resonant with Reality—that is, healthier — it becomes Unified, and thus *transparent*, revealing the underlying strata of Reality, thereby allowing other layers of Reality to be experienced and perceived. Then we manifest the ego as part of the Real Self and not as either "The Only Thing" or as an opponent to the Real Self.

One way we create artifacts is to take things out of context. This is done by the ego, which itself is— in its unhealed state—always out of context. In this way we lose the seamless, constantly moving and pulsating world for a static snapshot of something that has already passed.

To someone *within* the unhealed paradigm, that is, *within the artifact*, all the rules within that world are self-consistent, and the reality of the system is unquestioned.

While we usually associate this behavior with psychotic states, in reality it is true of all trance states, including the trance state that most of humanity finds itself in, wherein this piecemeal quality of the world seems correct: Self is seen as opposed to other; happiness, opposed to sorrow; and life, opposed to death.

This self-limiting and insular consciousness becomes a center of gravity, which is the theme of the system, when the system is viewed through this lens.

This is true whether we are talking about a physical, psychological, philosophical, or spiritual system. The fractured, artifact-aspect of consciousness cannot comprehend how to go further or beyond: An implacable, impenetrable law stands between it and Freedom.

While psychologically I would call this "the ego," in the physical universe, I would call this limiting paradigm "The Speed of Light."

Within this paradigm things are internally consistent, and run smoothly. There is even room for endless enlargement, exploration, and discussion. A certain level of Creation is possible here, and as in a dream, much can be garnered and experienced. But ultimately, it is still a dream. The Kabbalah calls this level of creation *"Something from Something"*; that is, we can make things with the things already there.

Going to a deeper or higher level of Creation, what the Kabbalah calls "Something from Nothing," would entail breaking this barrier, something that the self-consistent rules of this universe say is impossible. Thus the stage is set for the first pulsatory movement of the world to be felt, as this hard-won state of Wholeness becomes the very trap we sought to escape.

This trap may be described as *"rudra-ego"; that is, the ego which has become as big as the Universe; that is, as big as the system it is describing.*

We now exist in a state of completeness which makes all further Creation subject to the laws of that system or universe.

In this way, in its turn, this very coherence becomes its opposite: Instead of Freedom, it ends or limits further radical Creation. Coherence has become its own jailer.

Only by going faster than The Speed of Light, being willing to leave the Completeness and enter the Unknown, can we enter into a new paradigm and, along with it, a new perspective.

To find something truly New, or to see a deeper level hidden by the current Unity this universe presents to our minds, we must go faster than The Speed of Light; that is, we must leave the paradigm which formerly brought a sense of wholeness. We are talking here about psychological and perceptual Newness; we are talking about an original moment of Creation.

When a current level of Wholeness "solidifies" into a new limitation, then all of the creation that proceeds from that point on is "Something from Something."

We might also call this the Relativistic World.

Kabbalistically speaking, we call this a "yesh." Yesh means "something," as in *yesh-mi-yesh*, something from something.

This is a secondary level of creation, a level that is on its way to becoming an artifact. In this level, we create by increment and comparison. No new paradigm is found or explored. In fact, from the point of view of a Wholeness, which in its turn has become a *yesh*, new paradigms are resisted as assaults on the "The Truth." In this way, the former wholeness becomes turbulent and new artifacts are created.

In the Kabbalah, *yesh-mi-yesh* (*Something from Something*) is connected with the universe of Yitzerah, the psychological and symbolic universe. We are in this universe whenever we are exploring the *meaning* of the things (whether physical, emotional, or spiritual) around us. In this universe, things always relate to *other* things, and our intelligence is the intelligence of *comparison*.

The creation of Something from Something is the creation that happens in this milieu, and to go to a level of *new* creation, we must leave Yitzerah for the next deeper, more integrated universe, the universe of Briah.

In the universe of Briah, things are Themselves and are not symbolic. Essence is the ruling paradigm, and not meaning per se. Meaning rests in the Things Themselves, and the organizing principle is not the same as in other levels of creation. This is why the motto of this universe is Something from Nothing. *Nothing* here means "without concept."

While this statement may seem simple, the *experience* of relating to the world from this perspective is profound: Limitations dictated by the paradigm of the former Wholeness give way to Freedom, and the Self-Illuminating Light of the World begins to spring forth. Things are self-illuminating because— paradoxically—they light their own way *because* they are part of everything else. Because they are part of everything else, a Light springs up, which makes them Unique.

In our everyday universe of Asiyah-*Completeness*— which is the Wholeness that has become a trance and therefore an artifact that limits the perception of Reality—there is such a thing as *information*. This information is placed antithetically against chaos, as order is placed in opposition to *dis*-order.

But because all of the Universes (or: all of Reality, or: the All of God) are not really separate, but only appear so to the ego, which takes things out of context, aspects of deeper Realities seep through to our Asiyatic world upon close examination.

To use a Buddhist concept, we might call this moment the moment of realizing the first of Buddha's Noble Truths: *The world is suffering.* This suffering, which the ego does not want to see or even accept as a real and inviolate component of the world, but only as something to be escaped from, is the irreconcilable element that destroys the ego's conventional journey and leads it first to despair, next to Chaos-Creativity, and finally to Re-Birth.

These anomalies in our physical, psychological, and spiritual world are really gateways to the New. It is by noticing these anomalies that we begin to see the shadows of the Real. For example scientists have found that adding random noise to a system often lets the information being presented by that transmission get through more clearly. In the early days of telephony, much effort went into looking at the fundamental difference between information—say a voice—and noise—the static on the telephone line. Much to the surprise of some, it was found that in certain cases if some random noise was added back into the system, the sound of the voice was clearer. The same process was found to hold true in systems that transmitted pictures.

What is it about randomness that somehow acts as a *support* for the information? Is chaos somehow *part of order?*

Another example: How is it possible for quanta to communicate instantaneously over any distance, thereby breaking the speed of light barrier? For instance, if you create two photons and send them off in different directions and polarize the spin of one of them, the second photon—*upon examination*—will show the same spin.

Physicists have reconciled this anomaly by saying that what is being communicated *is not information*, but a form of non-information.

Yet, it is the experience of spiritually minded people that faster-than-light communication goes on all the time through telepathic communication, long-distance healing and so on. How can we reconcile these two views?

Another example: DNA research has mostly been concentrated on the amino acid sequences. Understanding the significance of these coding regions of DNA has brought profound under-standing and the ability to manipulate sequences with surprising understanding and powerful practical implications. Yet most of the DNA in the cell is *not in* recognizable pairings of amino acids, but in sequences that most geneticists have called "junk DNA," meaning that they have no meaning (and can be ignored!).

Recently, however, some researchers have noted that there is a sequence or order within the junk DNA, but that it is *statistical* and *linguistic* and follows the rules of natural languages rather than the rules of codes. To quote from a scientific report:

> "Stretches of seemingly meaningless DNA separate genes. Gibberish can also lie between coded regions within a gene. Long ignored as "junk," this noncoding DNA nevertheless caries its own message...(in the form of) languagelike properties.... Coding regions are just that: codes, not languages. One mistake, and the code will be misread. In contrast, because of...redundancy, the noncoding regions—like languages—can contain a mistake and still be understood. Also, the frequency with which various three-, four-, five-, six-, seven-, and eight-base pair patterns appear in noncoding regions varies **just as the frequency of words in a language does.**"

So a different paradigm lurks below the surface of meaning.

What is beginning to happen in these instances is that dearly held paradigms are eroding under our eyes.

There is enormous resistance to these changes in perspective. Now, new disciplines such as chaos and complexity theory are beginning to illuminate much deeper strata of how our universe works. Chaos theory has shown us that not only do so-called chaotic systems have order within them (albeit of a different type) but that this approach to regularity is often the one preferred by biological systems. So disorder and order are here not so far apart.

Kabbalists have always been *very* close readers of the Torah, seeing in each anomaly, in each seemingly unclear phrase, the Light of Heaven shining through a glass darkly. It is to bathe in that light, to find it, work with it, and live it, that kabbalists were born. Because the Torah is a language and not *only a code*, the deeper messages can be found throughout and rise to the surface in many places after careful study.

In the Torah, specifically in *Bereshit-Genesis*, there is a description of the first moments of Creation. To quote:

> *In the beginning, God created*
> *the heaven and the earth.*
> *Now the earth was unformed and void*
> *and darkness was upon the face of the deep*

and the spirit of God hovered over
the face of the waters.
And God said: Let there be Light.
And there was Light.

The words *unformed and void* are translations of the Hebrew words *tohu v-bohu.*

Formlessness *and* void: Why does the Torah need to use both words when one would do?

To the mind caught only on the level of relative-creation called Something from Something, this passage is about nothingness *versus* somethingness: First there was nothing, chaos, emptiness, and next—after God spoke, *after the Creative moment,* "Something" appeared, in this case: Light. But really this passage is about *the process of Creation,* which, in a non-relativistic way, *includes disorder, formlessness, voidness, and chaos as part of its Creativity.*

This passage says in effect, that these conditions are <u>vital to this level of Creation,</u> the Creation of Something from Nothing.

So speaking from an informational point of view, the relativistic, comparative mind says, *tohu v-bohu* contained no information. Then, when God speaks, *information appears.*

This is the type of limitation I call The Speed of Light. It is not incorrect *within* the paradigm, but it *ultimately* is, in that it is *limited*. Yet it is promoted as "the truth."

God, Reality, the Source of All, refuses however, to abide in this limitation.

From the Briatic point of view, tohu and bohu are yet *another self-limiting level of completeness, a level that— in its turn—disappears to uncover yet another level of Creation. Experiencing formlessness and void, vividly, without fear, but with abiding faith, is the only way to see the Essential Quality of this state of being.*

Anyone who has ever created an artistic product or who has meditated has been faced with this moment of surrender, where the ego simply cannot continue its program of control, and a new level of awareness and surrender to the process of Life must unfold.

Again, this can be seen only as the ego level of awareness is seen to be just that: not Reality but only a level. In this way, the artifact of the ego becomes transparent as the turbulence subsides.

It is only by giving up the struggle to reconcile tohu v-bohu <u>within</u> the framework of Yetzirah, (which we might call here the <u>former</u> Wholeness, or The Speed of Light) and entering it with complete vividness, that *movement toward a new paradigm, in which information is not pitted against non-information, can occur.*

This is a form of dying to one version of Reality, which also entails a re-entry into the new level of existence after a period tohu v-bohu. We might call this *being born again:*

This is true reincarnation.

(The connection to what "died" in the lower level of understanding, and what was "re-born" in the new level of understanding, after the dissolution of form and the discontinuity of personality, is a clearer picture of what gets carried forward in physical death: a kernel that is the same, but in different packaging. It is not personality per se that gets carried forward....)

Any Creation that is of the Divine Level must go through *tohu and bohu* to arrive there.

(Both tohu and bohu are needed because each describes a different quality of the Emptiness that is necessary for the Creative State. The Torah says "formless and void," in that one quality denotes the lack of ḥesed, which gives relativistic creation its radiative aspect, and the other denotes gevurah, which gives the universe the quality of All-at-One-ment, without which ḥesed could not radiate. Both sephirotic qualities are needed to create the Light spoken about here. This is a relativistic light, however,

which the Zohar calls, "the light of the eye." It is the light that can be comprehended by the very fact of its separation from the Source of All. It is light that exists in the comparison between this *and* that. *An earlier non-dualistic Light, which is described as "darkness," existed well before this moment and emerges from Keter, or the Divine Will. This type of Creation is incomprehensible to humans, but nevertheless stands as the Foundation for all subsequent Creation.)*

[The Set of the World] describes the condition that exists when the world itself and everything in it is held as a Completeness; when all Relativistic concerns are put aside, and the way is open for the apprehension of Divine Creation. It appears at the moment when neither duality nor Oneness are an obstacle. It is the moment the world is taken *as it is and bracketed so that both its Wholeness* <u>and its limitation</u> *can be seen.*

By bracketing the world, we are saying that we understand its limitations and accept them, and, by taking the world as a whole, we understand its Completeness, but are not entranced by it nor limited by it.

Vividly holding this *bracketed* Completeness, we leave room for another level of Radical Creation to emerge, Creation that does not—as of yet—fit in with the metaphoric Speed of Light as the self-limiting paradigm of the universe as seen from the vantage point of late twentieth-century humanity.

The experiments I would like to describe in the following pages are built on this foundation, and take these understandings as their starting point.

PART TWO

"One day I was walking in the desert and I beheld a tree, beautiful to look upon, and beneath it a cavern. I approached it and found that from the cavern issued a profusion of sweet odors. I plucked up courage and entered the cavern. I descended a number of steps which brought me to a place where there were many trees, and savours of overpowering sweetness. There I saw a man who held a scepter in his hand, standing at a place where the trees parted. When he saw me he was astonished and came up to me. "Who art thou, and what doest thou here?" he demanded. I was frightened exceedingly and said: "Sir, I am one of the Fellowship. I noticed this place in the desert, and so I entered." Said he: "As thou art one of the Fellowship, take this bundle of writings and give it to the members of the Fellowship, to those who know the mystery of the spirits of the righteous ones."

Zohar, Shemoth, Section 2, Page 13a

I would like to re-state some of the ideas we have already talked about from another point of view:

The purpose of alchemy is to turn each thing into its essence, rather than to turn one thing into another. That is: The purpose of alchemy is to take something that is a "thing" or *yesh*, which is to say, part of causal or comparative creation—a *skandas* in the Buddhist tradition—and turn it into intelligence of the heart, which is to say, its essence or True Self.

To help each thing find its essence is the purpose of alchemy. In this way, when we hold an emotional state within ourselves, neither suppressing it nor expressing it (which can be done only after the earlier psychological work is finished) this "thing" (the emotional state or feeling) changes back to its original form, its essence. In this case it becomes free and does not exist in reaction *to*, or in a reaction formation *against,* anything else.

It is in this spirit that we hold the world in the state of consciousness I call [The Set of the World].

In chess we have causality created by many different forces; in Go we have causality that results from a constantly repeating pattern, which is simultaneously free and unknowable.

So patterns are formed in a basic framework with singular and simple rules: All stones (Go pieces) have the same quality and powers and are differentiated and opposed only because of their different colors. All the subsequent drama is formed out of this simple but profound beginning.

In Asiyah, we have not yet even reached the stage where forces have become *things*. In the Asiyatic universe there are forces, psychological drives, instincts and so on, which drive our psychology in ways that are fundamentally unconscious for us.

It is a mark of great achievement when these forces become *yesh*, in the sense that the completely penetrating forces have somewhat solidified and become separate enough to coalesce into their actual forms, in which case we do not have to identify with them because they now have their own identity, which is separate from our sense of self.

As these pseudo-wholenesses are broken up, we begin to see that they are patterns and fragments, and not true Wholenesses or Whole Things in and of themselves.

It is at this point that the work of Briah begins: When we begin *staying with these yesh without trying to escape the form-anxiety that arises from our interactions with them*, there is the release of energy we are going to term "the burning."

In this state it is impossible either to move or not move, actualize yourself or defend yourself, run or stand still. You are what you are, when you are, where you are.

After that stage is accepted, the particular universe wherein the difficult force or emotional problem was found becomes harmonized into its fundamental structure; that is, *the essential characteristic of that universe, when there is no turbulence, emerges.*

In Yetzirah, this fundamental nature is *compassion* and *love.*

When we have done this work, our interactions with the world do not create karma but lessen it. Another way to say this: The emotion, once brought back to intelligence-of-the-heart (the non-comparative, non-dualistic combination of Heart and Mind), travels at the same "speed" as karma, and therefore is not affected by it, in the same way that someone riding a wave is not thrown over or hurt by the wave. The wave still exists (as does the difficult force or *yesh*), but we participate in its movement economically, exploring the essence of being human and all that that contains.

To experience [The Set of the World] it is necessary first to move with the world-as-a-force and into the transitional state where we do not have to identify with the world completely; that is, to the state wherein we can see the world as-it-is, accepting all the forces and things, and by bracketing them hold the world in its Wholeness, along with it limitations.

We must fundamentally accept that we are entering an Unknown (we do not bracket the world as something Known exclusively, but as something Knowable *and* Unknowable) and that as we enter this Unknown it becomes a *Known*. And that each Known leads to a yet deeper *Unknown* and so on.

In this way, each successive Unknown has more power to engender Wholeness.

This alternating dance is one of the primary conditions of a universe that emerged from Oneness into Duality, and the pulsatory feeling we get from this movement into Reality never leaves us, but deepens, until we could call it the Breathing of the World. This pulsation is the Heartbeat of this Universe, and is found on all levels of Creation.

In our relationship with the sephirot, we must settle into the Unknown as well as the Known feeling of cleaving. Each successive deepening of the Known/Unknown Relationship increases *Presence-Intention (kavannah)* until we are dealing with the Presence of God.

So we cleave to the Unknown/Known Wholeness. We accept and surrender, yet remain emerged, yet nameless, held and holding [The Set of the World].

[The Set of the World] originally began as an experiment in communication.

I understood that information (communication) that is constructed from the arrangement of quantum particles, whether electrons or photons, will be subject to quantum laws and hence limited by The Speed of Light as I have defined that concept metaphorically.

In order to go beyond that paradigm, it would be necessary for the communication to take place in a milieu of information that is beyond or above the arrangement of quanta, whether in the form of waves or particles.

When one holds [The Set of the World], the world in every manifestation becomes *information*. That set of information becomes an integral unit in and of itself, beyond the meaning or energy of the individual members of the set. It is not information *about something,* so much as the *concept* of information as a Whole.

In kabbalistic language, the *parztufim* are arrangements of *sephirot* that profoundly increase and change the already profound messages of these entities by arraying them in structures that impart new levels of information and are in fact themselves *information.*

This is true because the level of relationship is even more developed in the partzufic personae.

Thus, the living cell is greater than the sum of its parts; the poem, more than a series of words and definitions; the tree, more than its leaves and wood; a person, more than intricate chemical combinations which themselves cannot think or feel.

When one holds [The Set of the World], the world becomes information and that information becomes a new organism, an organism that is not confined by The Speed of Light.

We are now no longer limited by the interaction of quanta, but by an association that is *the product of the interaction and arrangement of quantum particles or forces.*

We are in essence at a finer wavelength, in the same way that *thought* is finer than written letters, and neutrinos are finer than steel.

It became apparent to me that one type of information—perhaps a special type—could be sent as a "pulse" through the world held as a Whole; that is, the set, which is a set of infinity, containing the manifest and unmanifest, the known *and* the unknown; the knowable and the unknowable: [The Set of the World].

This *pulse* or "push" embodies the new information being sent through the information of [The Set of the World]; and is created by one Wholeness interacting with another Wholeness.

In the experiments I have conducted from this Position, I have stood "outside" [The Set of the World] and *pushed.*

This "pushing" is non-dual: It is not the feeling of *pushing* "something" or "against something." We might say that it is not pushing which is born of the action of one force *upon* another, but of the innate pulsatory movement of Knowns turning into Unknowns.

It is intentional and efforted, but not born of struggle.

When the world is held in brackets, the pulse of this *pushing* goes evenly through it. It *seems* radiative, but it goes in two directions at once.

If I posit another person *outside (yet part of)* [The Set of the World], this pulse seems to "reach" them and me *at the same moment.* There is also a feeling of the person and myself, both of whom stand "outside" of the [The Set of the World] (and yet are part of it), as being the same *Being.*

There is the distinct feeling of something moving in two directions at once, something that does not take time (as in radiative movement), and that arrives simultaneously at both destinations.

While this phenomena is quite remarkable and unsettling for our three-dimensional body and consciousness, it is possible that it merely reflects the underlying geometry of space, a geometry which is invisible in its actual form from our limited perspective, but which nonetheless manifests here as the artifact of a higher-dimensional truth.

William Thurston, Jeffrey Weeks and others are mathematicians who have been studying new topological models for the space of our universe. Specifically, these investigators have begun thinking about the shape of the universe as hyperbolic geometric structures called three-dimensional polyhedrons.

These models allow for a universe that is negatively curved, yet finite.

I would like to quote from an article in *Science News* (2/21/98):

> *[To imagine a three-dimensional manifold, we could imagine] gluing together the sides of a rubbery rectangle. For example, a torus is simply a rectangle with opposite sides glued together. The first gluing creates a tube, and the second gluing connects the two ends of the tube to form a ring.*
>
> *The same idea can be generalized to describe a three-dimensional manifold. For instance, one can try to imagine gluing together the opposite faces of a flexible cube to produce a hypertorus—the three-dimensional equivalent of a doughnut surface.*
>
> *Thurston and Weeks were key figures in the development of a comprehensive catalog of closed three-dimensional manifolds, most of which appear to have a hyperbolic*

geometric structure. These weird shapes can be understood in terms of three-dimensional polyhedrons whose faces are glued together to create finite, multiply-connected spaces.

My first diagram of the experience of working with [The Set of the World] was this:

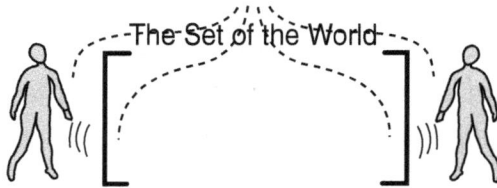

It is possible that what I am really experiencing is the falling away of three-dimensional consciousness, in favor of the "leaking through" of higher-dimensional geometry, in which case the diagram below might express this experience more faithfully.

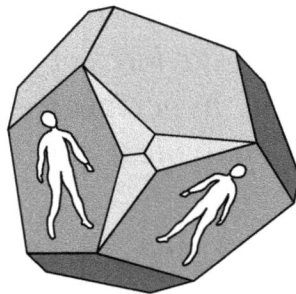

The two faces indicated, while separated in three-dimensions, are really contiguous in higher-dimensions. Thus the apparent "splitting" or "arriving" at two places at once is really an expression of some innate geometry.

Part Three

Memory is motionless.
  −Bachelard

Finally, I would like to look at some of these ideas from yet another Kabbalistic perspective.

1. *Gevurah* is Infinite (for all practical purposes) yet it is not *radiative. We might therefore call it At-One-Ment, that Quality which is Everywhere, but which has Never Arrived, Never Gone, yet is ultimately flexible and alive and pulsating (but not in a radiative or time-bound way).*

2. *Nega*-gevurah is All-at-Onement which is frozen, not moving, because it is directed and contained by memory.

3. In Asiyah, memory is in the past, and its influence on the future is not clearly seen.

4. In Yetzirah, memory is fluid, and "memories" are constructs out of time but in space; that is, objects, which show up in various times: past, present, and future.

5. In Briah, *nega*-gevurah becomes increasingly hard to find because its unity with hesed is more profound. *Nega*-gevurah is found only when

gevurah is disassociated from ḥesed. Instead of finding *nega*-gevurah, we see gevurah *moving*. This quality of *movingness* is not the same as ḥesed's radiative outward movement, but a kind of scaffolding which awaits ḥesed's radiative movement, but unlike a human scaffolding, incorporates an indefinable quality of *motion* in itself. This *movingness* is an expression of gevurah's unity with ḥesed's outward flow at this level of being.

6. So objects of all kinds are frozen time, space in which "old time" is continuous and still persistent.

7. This includes psychological objects.

8. These persistent objects create *habit*, as moving, living time patterns itself around the seeds of the past.

9. The deeper the object is in the structure of the universe (and the more convincing its reality is to our psyche), the more persistent it is, and the more new fresh time forms itself around it, adheres to it, and becomes like it. Reality patterns itself around the persistent object.

10. Healing is always moving upward or inward through the universes, toward more freedom and less objectification.

11. The ego itself is the *Prime Pattern* around which we construct a "snapshot-self," the psychological and temporal space of our lives. The ego is our most persistent object.

12. We thereby reduce the free movement of conditions which are our birthright.

13. On the positive side, when we completely crystallize out *(or hold)* a psychological/spiritual difficulty or concept, we see its object-ness *clearly;* that is, its entirety becomes an object within the *next* higher setting or universe. It ceases being a force.

14. Once seen, it has much less control over our lives. It ceases to attract the same amount of our inner forces; it cannot co-opt them, to build— like viruses—more of itself.

15. In diagnosis, even when we honestly choose a healing that has some objectification, if it is a deeper, *truer* object, time and space begin to form themselves around it, and a new, dynamic movement can take place. We call this healing.

16. To be completely free is to have seen the *Prime Pattern* clearly and to be free to form around it or not, as we wish.

17. Rivers flow through the countryside, passing brown leaves fallen from trees, and rocky outcroppings, and mossy rocks. We see occasional pieces of trash, wet with rain, left there by someone escaping themselves through unconsciousness, someone for whom [The Set of the World] is invisible.

18. These rivers are ourselves. These rocks, our hands. All is part of the pattern we flow with and melt with, moving toward the Sea. Gevurah cannot help but unite with ḥesed: Love finds love in freedom. It is Freedom that finds Liberation.

THE MASTER OF HIDDENNESS

A Practical Commentary on the
Prayer *Adon Olam* for the Restoration of
Our Original Connection to God

JASON SHULMAN

My heart needs to praise You
But I am unable.
If only my understanding were
as spacious as Solomon's:
Without his open wisdom
I cannot tell of Your wonders
and goodness, these things You
have made for me and all
the world.
Without You there is only hopelessness
and no bedrock to support
and sustain the tired world.
I am a lost child...
No: I am cast upon You,
and want only You,
You who hold
in Your hand the spirit within
every living thing,
You who breathe the breath
that becomes
the world.

Solomon ibn Gabirol
(version by JS)

אֲדוֹן עוֹלָם אֲשֶׁר מָלַךְ, בְּטֶרֶם כָּל
יְצוּר נִבְרָא. לְעֵת נַעֲשָׂה בְחֶפְצוֹ
כֹּל, אֲזַי מֶלֶךְ שְׁמוֹ נִקְרָא. וְאַחֲרֵי
כִּכְלוֹת הַכֹּל, לְבַדּוֹ יִמְלוֹךְ נוֹרָא.
וְהוּא הָיָה וְהוּא הֹוֶה, וְהוּא יִהְיֶה
בְּתִפְאָרָה. וְהוּא אֶחָד וְאֵין שֵׁנִי,
לְהַמְשִׁיל לוֹ לְהַחְבִּירָה. בְּלִי רֵאשִׁית
בְּלִי תַכְלִית, וְלוֹ הָעֹז וְהַמִּשְׂרָה. וְהוּא
אֵלִי וְחַי גֹּאֲלִי, וְצוּר חֶבְלִי בְּעֵת צָרָה.
וְהוּא נִסִּי וּמָנוֹס לִי, מְנָת כּוֹסִי בְּיוֹם
אֶקְרָא. בְּיָדוֹ אַפְקִיד רוּחִי, בְּעֵת אִישַׁן
וְאָעִירָה. וְעִם רוּחִי גְוִיָּתִי, יְיָ לִי וְלֹא
אִירָא:

Introduction

The prayer *Adon Olam* begins with the words "Master of the World." Who is this Master and what is the world? The *Zohar* teaches us that this Master is the "Mysterious Unknown," and that the World is an expression of God's Unknowable Unity.

In other places—especially in the daily liturgy—God is also described as *Mighty, Awesome, Guardian, Merciful One, Lord, Deliverer* and so on.

Which God is it that we are relating to when we love God and hate people? Which God is it that is in our hearts when we have feuds over our understanding and interpretations of basic scriptures and consign to Hell those we do not agree with? Which God do we have when we have "God on our side?"

The *Shema,* the great *mantra* of Judaism, teaches us that God is only One. This means that to live a Godly life, we must relate to All of God: the Knowable *and* the Unknowable, the Mysterious *and* the Plain, the Awesome One *and* the Intimate One.

Because we are principally *egoic* creatures; that is, beings for whom the *individual self* ranks high in importance, we tend to see only the part of Life that suits the needs of this limited perspective. And in any case, how could we possibly relate to something that is beyond human comprehension? How can we *know* the Unknowable?

It is my feeling that not only is this possible, but vital. When we relate to only one portion of who God is, we remake God in our own image; we turn God into something that allows us to continue the *naming of the world in our own image.* This continued fragmentation is at once our glory and our despair. Our glory because it is a sign of our intelligence and ability to use the world God gave us; our despair because it destroys the Wholeness of which we are made. And without this Wholeness we are half human beings, beings who only search for God, but never find Him.

Each day we pray and the words often slip by unnoticed. We miss the clues that the prayers contain which could allow us to exist in the undivided state, the state that heals all the fracturing within us and allows us to be with God in the highest condition. Without this *d'aat,* this knowledge or connection, God only becomes bigger and more distant, and we, smaller and more insignificant, creating an unbridgeable gap between Creator and Created.

But the Kabbalah teaches us that we are not insignificant, and that contrary to that view, our every action is important, making God's Life manifest here on earth. It is important to understand that it is the Unknowable aspect of God that makes this co-creation possible. Our God is a living God only to the extent that we understand the Undivided One, the One Who is Singular.

It is the obligation of every seeker of God not to be stopped by the difficulty the ego presents. To be men and women of God means to love with our *entire* being, and not with just the parts we understand or like.

How do we love with the parts of ourselves that are still in confusion or darkness? How do we love with the parts of ourselves that still suffer? In short, how do we love God, jump into God, exist in God, make manifest through our daily actions the activity of God, and still be who we are: imperfect human beings whose understanding is small?

A deeper reading of our prayers can show us the way. Many of these prayers are by unknown authors; some, like *Adon Olam*, are attributed to specific people. But all of these prayers were written by men and women who dared and persevered to know God. They tried to put the Ineffable into words and into their lives.

In this small book, I would like to retrace the steps of *Adon Olam*, taking the reader from the outer meaning of the words to the inner experience, and eventually, through the use of several exercises contained in the text, to the Wordless Place where God awaits.

Then, returning from a glimpse of the Great Silence, we can make our life here on earth more like our Father's life in Heaven, and see God in every shining face.

I consider this a completely practical book, a small book for people who want the tools to create their own map to Heaven and who are willing to find that Heaven here on earth.

I once criticized someone who was making serious errors of judgment with their children. My criticism was accurate but ultimately unfair. Because I saw only what was wrong and did nothing to decrease the separation between me and this person, the final effect of my comments could only have pushed this person further and further into despair: After all, someplace in their body, mind, and soul, they already knew they were doing wrong. It was only when I returned to the Source of my Being that I knew that the root cause of this person's actions was their injured dignity; the fact that their own specialness and beauty had been violated again and again as a child. Without that wound, they could never act as they had acted, and without their undisclosed greatness and unmanifest closeness to God, they could never have felt ashamed and hurt by their own actions. So what they needed from me at that point was a pure apology, with no strings attached, with no further comment about their parenting skills. I said to them, "I'm sorry I spoke as I did. It was stupid and wrong." They were gracious enough to laugh and accept my apology.

When we use God to divide ourselves from others and not see the best in them (which does not mean not confronting evil when we see it), we are seeing only half of God, which is to say, we are not seeing God at all, and then we have no chance at all of accomplishing *tikkun-olam,* the healing of the world.

So let us read *Adon Olam* together, and be women and men of God together, and be willing to go from place to place and see God everywhere, for that is where He truly Is.

The Prayer

1 Lord of the Universe
2 Who reigned before anything was Created
3 At the time when by His will all things were made,
4 Then was His name proclaimed King.
5 And after all things shall cease to be,
6 The Awesome One will reign alone.
7 He was, He is, and He shall be in glory.
8 He is One, and there is no other to compare to Him,
9 To consort with Him.
10 Without beginning, without end,
11 Power and dominion belong to Him.
12 He is my God and my ever-living Redeemer,
13 The strength of my lot in time of distress.
14 He is my banner and my refuge,
15 My portion on the day I call.
16 Into His hand I entrust my spirit, when I sleep and when I wake.
17 And with my soul, my body too, the Lord is with me,
18 I shall not fear.

Praying

It is morning and I am praying.

I pray to remember God and I pray to forget myself.
I pray to remember the One who made me and of
whom I am truly a part, and also to forget the separate
one whose only memory is exile.

I know that people all over the world are suffering,
some from having no context into which to put their
human suffering; some because the suffering inherent
in being alive has been increased by the willful, blind
acts of others.

I know others are suffering because they think they
know God but know only a larger version of their
own unredeemed self. I know this not because I
disagree with their interpretations, but simply because
their actions increase the suffering and despair of others.

I augment reading the written prayers with my own
voice: I ask God to lessen the distance between me
and Him, a distance for which I know I am responsible.

I slow down and read each word. Sometimes I get to
read only one or two prayers in the morning, but I
get to love each word and learn.

A good prayer is a good teacher. It brings solace, attention, meaning, and insight. It is an endless meeting and an always deepening pool of water that takes me like a diver down to my essential liquid.

The untransformed ego is an ego in pain, no matter how hard it tries to hide this fact. To be essentially separate from the world—a world which is an expression of the Creator's unity—is to be in suffering, and that is the condition all of us find ourselves in, no matter who we are. In fact, in Buddhism the Buddha's first Noble Truth states that we must accept that suffering is our condition before we can move on to the understanding of how to alleviate suffering.

When I begin to read *Adon Olam*, I ask myself, "Who is reading these words?" I know the answer by how my bodymindspirit reacts: Do I feel smaller as I read the words? Do I feel more hopeful, closer to God, or more despairing because of my faults and imperfections? Do I receive more kindness from the words and, healed in that way, give more kindness to others? Or do I walk away in more rigid sorrow, feeling envious of others who I imagine have achieved a form of union I can never hope to experience?

I have learned from long experience how to tell who the reader is, and I have also found that this sorrowing child can be helped by actually understanding the words I am reading in a different way, a way that brings me into the Pure Present, which is the Time in which God appears as a palpable Presence.

And then, my ego, fearing banishment and at the same time hoping for some form of anesthesia that can quell its pain, is transformed into a friend who leads the way and then willingly steps aside so that it too can be in Light and come Home to its Origin.

From this perspective, *Adon Olam* is a ladder that reaches from wherever we are to God. It is a map written by someone who experienced the Settling-into-Place that is also called an awakening into God, and it calls to us each morning to make the world New.

Before the King

1 Lord of the Universe
2 Who reigned before anything was Created

Immediately the prayer calls to our limited self and asks us to be more.

When we speak to a Lord we must avert our eyes. Traditionally, we were not allowed to look upon the visage of even a human lord and therefore the image of a lord and a kneeling subject brings forth a feeling of separation: There is little commerce between these two.

This model of relationship makes room for *difference* and *awe,* but no room for *intimacy* and *understanding.* And what do we make of "universe," a word so large that we seem to be no part of it at all?

A Being that is Master of All This is someone who is the complete opposite of what we feel and experience ourselves to be: small beings who arrive here without knowing why and leave the same way. This is not the type of mastery we can have, and yet the ego keens to have this very thing it does not know how to achieve.

We find ourselves immediately on the outside looking in—from the perspective of the small self—the distance between ourselves and God growing fiercely moment by moment.

But the words *Master* and *Universe* can have an alternative translations:

Adon	**olam**	**asher**	**malach**
master	*of the universe*	*who*	*reigns*
possessor	*hiddenness*		

biterem	**kol**	**yitzir**	**neevra**
before	*any*	*formation*	*was created*
	all		

What is a Master of Hiddenness? Who is it who can *possess* Hiddenness?

To begin to understand that, we must understand more clearly how our usual consciousness works.

Kabbalah teaches us that the original act of creation was a kind of division: God *divided* Himself from the All in order to create a *vacated space* in which seemingly independent beings could exist outside the effulgence of God. This act of experiment, of mercy, of incomprehensibility, at the foundation of creation, is repeated in a fractal manner at every other level of creation, from material reality to consciousness.

Thus, this first act of *division* is replicated in our egos, which create the world anew each moment by a kind of imitation of God's creative process:

We *divide* the world each moment, and all of our typical understanding arises from our understanding of opposites.

In this way, to our usual consciousness, God's Light is the opposite of darkness. Everything that Light is stands in opposition to what darkness is. If Light is knowing, then darkness is the unknown; if Light is consciousness, then darkness is associated with the unconscious. In short, Light is all that we see as good; darkness all that we see as bad.

Light is the polar opposite of darkness.

But if we think for a moment of those times that we felt Whole, there is one thing that stands out: In those moments, *all of life* was somehow acceptable. That we suffered by being alive was part of life; that we had fear in our hearts was a tender thing; that we were often afraid of loving was understandable; that death was inevitable was a bittersweet tonic that made every moment precious.

We can say: To the Whole Self, this Self that seems to come of its own volition and leave the same way, Spiritual Light is not one half of an equation weighed down by its opposite.

Instead, it is the entirety of Creation Itself, the unfathomable Darkness and the Light united in an invisible but palpable luminosity.

This is not the usual way we see the world or God, and so to the ego it is incomprehensible. Even though we describe God as "unknowable," "beyond comprehension," and "mysterious," these words are never taken into the soul, since *it is still the little ego hearing them; they never sprout into the tree of life at the center of our being.*

Instead, the ego does with even these words what it does with all others: It splits them apart and says in essence, "God is great; I am nothing," and is left to travel the ensuing distance in either blind faith or despair…though we have so much more available to us.

But to take that journey we have to begin to give up one of the human powers that is intimately associated with our egos: the power to speak, define, and bring things into relief.

Language is usually ruled by the egoic function and in this way serves as a veil between us and the experience we so desperately need to be fully human. But paradoxically, we can use words to bring us to a clearer, more Whole place, though especially at first, the ego will not understand the sense and sentence of this new language.

For God is a God of All Places, and for God the quality of Hiddenness does not stand in opposition to Revelation. Hiddenness instead is the fountain from which all creation flows.

From the *Sefer ha-'Iyyun*: The Book of Contemplation (Verman):

> "...He comprises all sides, hidden and revealed. He begins above and ends below, and concludes before and behind, and right and left. He possesses the power of shape and the power of image and the power of form, which is not perceived. He is unique and his unity is revealed and covered, hidden and secret."

Since all things in Heaven and earth are One, the closer we look at earth, the more Heaven is revealed. As we look at the atomic level of things, the more "thing-ness" breaks down. Things unthinkable in the conglomerate world begin to disassemble at the quantum level: Photons that *appear* to be waves and particles simultaneously hide an even more hidden unity beneath these final appearances. In the psychological sphere, true looking is connected with true acceptance: seeing things as they are. And when we practice that, the hidden appears, not as something un-hidden or *revealed,* but simply as *itself.* It is then that we can *feel* the world in its Wholeness, and wordlessly know our part in it.

To be a Master of Hiddenness, God must hold hiddenness completely, without trying to change it. God must give hiddenness a Place to Be.

The *Zohar* also speaks of this Hiddenness:

> *"In the Beginning," when the will of the King began to take effect, he engraved signs into the heavenly sphere. Within the most hidden recess a dark flame issued from the mystery of Ain Sof, the Infinite, like a fog forming in the unformed—enclosed in the ring of that sphere, neither white nor black, neither red nor green, of no color whatever. Only after this flame began to assume size and dimension, did it produce radiant colors. From the innermost center of the flame sprang forth a well out of which colors issued and spread upon everything beneath, hidden in the mysterious hiddenness of Ain Sof.*

And:

> *R. Eleazar opened his discourse with the text: Lift up your eyes on high and see: who hath created these? (Is. XL, 26). "Lift up your eyes on high": to which place? To that place to which all eyes are turned, to wit, Petah 'Enaim ("eye-opener"). By doing so, you will know that it is the mysterious Ancient One, whose essence can be sought, but not*

81

*found, that created these: to wit, Mi (Who?), the
same who is called "from (Heb. mi) the extremity
of heaven on high," because everything is in His
power, and because He is ever to be sought, though
mysterious and unrevealable, since further we
cannot enquire. That extremity of heaven is called
Mi, but there is another lower extremity which is
called Mah (What?). The difference between the
two is this: The first is the real subject of enquiry,
but after a man by means of enquiry and reflection
has reached the utmost limit of knowledge, he
stops at Mah (What?), as if to say, what knowest
thou? what have thy searchings achieved?*

Mah? (What?) points at an object and thus is the outer
limit of what can be understood as knowledge by the
intellect alone.

Arriving here, at this last outpost of knowing, our
final *egoic* statement must be: "What have we really
achieved?" For wisdom, that non-place beyond
knowledge, is not found here.

This passage, then, is not only a statement of the need
for *general* humility, *but an expression of the limit of the
intellect's ability to understand the Unknowable Hiddenness
and a factual statement* of how the observer himself
must change for the world as a Whole to make sense.

And further:

> Then he said to me, "Master, the Holy One, blessed
> be He, had a deep secret which He at length
> revealed at the celestial Academy. It is this: When
> the most Mysterious wished to reveal Himself, He
> first produced a single point which was transmuted
> into a thought, and in this He executed
> innumerable designs and engraved innumerable
> gravings. He further graved within the sacred and
> mystic lamp a mystic and most holy design, which
> was a wondrous edifice issuing from the midst of
> thought. This is called MI, and was the beginning
> of the edifice, existent and non-existent, deep-
> buried, unknowable by name. It was only called
> MI (Who?). It desired to become manifest and to
> be called by name. It therefore clothed itself in a
> refulgent and precious garment and created ELeH
> (these), and ELeH acquired a name. The letters
> of the two words intermingled, forming the
> complete name ELoHIM (God).

(Advanced students of Integrated Kabbalistic Healing
will recognize here the origin of Threads, which come
from the realm of *ahdut ha-shaveh*/balanced unity.)

This passage is about the movement from the
unmanifest to the manifest. It shows how the essence
of God appears both in the manifest world—in one

form which can be Named—and in the *un*-manifest world, which the *Zohar* states can only be called Who?, the Who which has only One Answer. It also shows us how we can follow this echo of the Real Self from the manifest world back to the Hiddenness that is our origin.

Usually in prayers we deal with the manifest only, and the Names by which we commonly address God, such as *Elohim, Adonai, El Chai,* and so on, are the Names given to God after the *Ain Sof becomes manifest.*

Clearly, the manifest God is easier for human beings to relate to: We are a being and we like to relate to God as if God were only a being as well, this despite the "unnamable and unknowable" aspect of God.

But God cannot be limited to being a personality. He is that but much beyond that as well.

When we experience God only in the manifest form, we experience only one side of Creation. To experience the fullness of God, it is necessary to experience the One who is manifest *and* non-manifest.

This puts this type of exploration squarely outside the understanding and possibility of the ego, which exists only in the house of the personality. It is simply the wrong tool to explore Wholeness.

Adon Olam helps us experience the unmanifest.

Try this:

> *Sit quietly for a few moments. Thoughts will naturally arise in your mind. This is all right: The mind was made to make and contain thoughts.*
>
> *However, as each thought comes up from the depths of your mind, simply say, "Who?"*
>
> *At first, you will wait for an answer.*
>
> *Eventually an answer will come, when the discursive mind—the mind of the ego, which constantly discusses the world with itself—quiets down enough to hear the sound of the Still Small Voice. The answer will be the One who is questioning. It is God seeking God.*

The beginning of *Adon Olam* speaks not only to the Knowable and Nameable God, but also to the God before form. This is the God of the "higher extremity."

This is made even more clear because the Possessor of Hiddenness is defined as the "One who reigned before any formation (being, thing) was created." This is God before Time, before Names, before Speaking and Silence, and including all of these. *Adon Olam* is a hymn to this Placeless Place to which we are invited to go.

Prayers are activities and need to be tried out: When we say "Who?" to our most essential self we catch a glimpse of the Friend who asks of us only our Whole Heart. Say, "Who?" whole-heartedly, and you have a key to enter Heaven.

God's Desire

3 At the time when by His will all things were made,
4 Then was His name proclaimed King.
5 And after all things shall cease to be,
6 The Awesome One will reign alone.

We awake in the morning, called to consciousness by…something. It is the moment before we move to stretch our body out, and for a minute we do not know who we are.

When we are children, we often play with this moment, either upon waking or in the moments before we fall asleep. We don't know who we are, *and yet we exist.*

And then something changes. We move a leg, we realize we are lying *here* or *there,* we remember our name and with that, all the things we need to do, what we left unfinished, even the argument we had the night before, which remains with us, a dissonant, troublesome thing, where only moments before we were in the moment *before* happiness, a small but balanced bliss.

Where does the next thought come from? Usually our minds are too busy to see the ground of mind itself, that place which is apparent *between* thoughts. But when we quiet down we can see the mind as a kind of soft darkness.

Then: a thought.

Here, *Adon Olam* is *thinking*. The prayer begins in the moment *before time*, before anything was created, and moves to the next—or the first—moment.

"At the time when by His Will..."

Now we are told that *time* and *His Will* somehow appear together, mutually arising from a Place that precedes any naming, a Place where Hiddenness rules and is the wellspring of all that is yet to come. At this moment in the prayer, the World is about to come into being.

But why is this so? For the child in bed and for God in Heaven, why does this First Thought arise? This Thought that changes everything? What is God's Plan? And why, with the Creation of Time and the arising of Will, does God become a King and rule forever?

Again, from the egoic point of view, God shows Himself to be a King and—from the point of view of the ego—kings can do whatever they want, including rule forever. So from the perspective of this small consciousness, this passage is about *power.*

But from the *non-egoic* point of view, this passage is about a type of Will the ego does not understand: a Will that has no object, and whose power comes from its total Freedom and its total pleasure in the act of Creation.

When we practiced saying, "Mi?" (Who?) to each of
our thoughts and feelings, a point came when the
thoughts we were addressing became less important
than the Who? itself, until finally the Who? stood
alone, and something new came into our awareness,
a subtle glow that was both light and darkness at the
same time.

If we apply this non-dual, non-polar understanding
and body-sense to the word "will," we will begin to
have some idea of God's Will and how it brings all
things into existence at once. And experiencing this
unique will lets us move from the manifest to the
un-manifest, from the world as it is now to what was
before, thereby including both aspects, and in this way
cleaving more closely to a singular God.

In Adon Olam, the word "(bi)chephtzo" is used to
designate a kind of will associated with desire and with
pleasure. If we substitute another word, kavvanah,
which is also translated as will, devotion, or intention,
we can begin to have some idea of what this desire or
will is truly like, a Will or Desire that needs no
relationship to an object in order to exist. God's Will.
Paradoxically, only by understanding Divine Will can
we make sense of our own. Only by understanding
Divine kavvanah, can we begin to live a life where
everything comes into being fresh and alive, in the

way it springs into existence as described in these lines of *Adon Olam*.

Although *kavvanah* is usually translated as *focus* or *attention* or *will*, I would like to redefine it, because a deeper and truer understanding of this word and the quality it brings can help us liberate ourselves from our internal exile.

This place of exile is something we all know about. The feeling that emotionally and spiritually we are not yet at the place we feel we should be; the deeply held belief that somehow we are not enough as we are, and that God is something or someone far away who we must search and search for.

Often *kavvanah* is described as one of the most important qualities we need to bring to spiritual activity to make it effective.

In other words: If you practice the violin with focus and dedication, you are simply going to get better at playing it, until one day, from the mass of movements and sounds there comes *music*.

And the same attitude is carried forward to spiritual matters: If you approach your spiritual practice with the qualities of *devotion, focus,* and *attention*, whether your practice is prayer, yoga, meditation, or following the path of commandments, you are going to get better at what you do, and the thought is: *getting better at those things, will bring you closer to God.*

There is no question that most people who begin a spiritual path go through a stage where they are trying to perfect their practice: They add more discipline; they spend a longer amount of time doing their practice; they are more faithful to it, and so on.

We say to ourselves: If I am better at *my practice,* then I am going to make headway; I am going to get closer to God, or the Source, or Ultimate Reality, or whatever we call it.

The unspoken understanding here is this: *Kavvanah* is *something* I will *bring* **to** my practice to **improve** it, and **it** *will then improve* **me.**

So, from this way of looking at *kavvanah,* it is a sort of home-improvement project, where we are the builder, and what we are building is our home in Heaven.

Looked at from this point of view, *kavvanah* is mainly *a specific form of effort* we bring to our spiritual enterprise, a *tool* that will help us lift a heavier load.

But while this type of effort seems almost always to help us with certain types of tasks, like learning a language or a new instrument for example, with spiritual development this is not always the case.

In fact, we have all found, as beings on a spiritual quest, that paradoxically enough, *effort* is exactly what we sometimes need to *get rid of* to make any real progress. Effort is sometimes tied up with our ego's limited view of the spiritual path and serves to strengthen the parts of our ego we should actually be trying to diminish.

Those parts are, for example:

self-will (versus surrender)
my way (as opposed to God's way)
fear (instead of trust)
perfectionism (versus real life)
...and so on.

So what else can *kavvanah* be?

Our usual understanding of *kavvanah* maintains a very subtle but powerful split, a split that is reinforced by our language, which has a strong *subject versus object* bias, and in turn by our consciousness, which is shaped by language.

In this way of thinking, *kavvanah* is an *objective action* that is performed *on a subject.*

It is some *thing,* some procedure or something added that *makes something we are already doing* <u>better</u>. *It's like the secret, active ingredient.*

This way of looking at things reinforces the *ego's view of the world*, which is: a basic separation between ourselves and what we want, in this case, God. The subject/object split says, "God is out there, contained in the ultimate perfection of my practice, and *kavvanah* is something that will help me get *from here to there.*

In a sense, this world view believes God is contained—somehow—in the perfection of the practice itself.

There is a story about this in the Torah, where Jacob is bewildered by his own consciousness, which made him think that God was far away:

> And Jacob went out from Beersheba, and went toward Haran. And he lighted upon a certain place, and remained there all night, because the sun was set; and he took of the stones of that place, and put them for his pillows, and lay down in that place to sleep.
>
> And he dreamed, and behold! A ladder was set up on the earth, and the top of it reached to heaven; and behold the angels of God ascending and descending on it. And, behold! The Lord stood above it, and said, I am the Lord God of Abraham your father, and the God of Isaac; the land on which you lie, to you will I give it, and to your

seed. And your seed shall be as the dust of the earth, and you shall spread abroad to the west, and to the east, and to the north, and to the south; and in you and in your seed shall all the families of the earth be blessed. And, behold, **I am with you, and will keep you in all places where you go,** *and will bring you back to this land; for I will not leave you, until I have done that about which I have spoken to you. And Jacob awoke from his sleep, and he said,* **Surely the Lord is in this place; and I knew it not.** *And he was afraid, and said, How awesome is this place! this is no other but the house of God, and this is the gate of heaven.*

One of the many things this story illustrates is Jacob's mystification that God was *in the very place that Jacob was.*

Jacob did not understand until that moment that *God was with him in every place*. That there was no place God was not.

Jacob's *ego*, the "I" that knew it not, could not fathom the immediacy of God. It created the illusion of a place that had no God or God's only being able to be in a "special place."

The ego's job is to keep us safe and make things happen *for us.*

Consequently, the ego *always* loves to exteriorize, to make separate, to differentiate, to create drama. It exists by virtue of its ability to split from the Self and engage in self-reflective observation.

The spirit, on the other hand, always likes to understand the Nearness of God, the Immanence of God, how we and the Holy are not really separate at all.

Our language helps us maintain the illusion that "God was not in this Place."

Scientists are beginning to understand that acquisition of language actually changes structures in the brain, and that these structural changes determine to some extent how we will see the world.

If our brains are structured differently, we will see the world differently.

So, the ego—which is to some extent created and maintained by language—has its supremacy reinforced by our use of language, which generates our world view.

But if we look to the roots of language, if we change the words we use to see the world, we have a way to see past the dualistic bias in our consciousness and see the world's underlying unity.

When we do not do that, for most of us the search for God takes on a distinctly dualistic flavor.

This dualistic drama is in keeping with the egoic psychic structures, which tell us that God is very far away and that we must practice to get to Him.
So we follow prescribed rules and hope to *purify*, until the *distance between ourselves and our goal (God) is lessened.*

This is the methodology of most esoteric paths, and it is necessary, but not for the reasons we usually think: that we can get to God solely by this method. It is necessary because we first need to create the ground to hold a new level of energy and consciousness and to help the ego understand that it is not the center of the universe so that it can let go to something more Whole.

The Way is about surrender.

But while this path of purification is important and even vital, this by itself is not enough. We must have an experience of life that is non-egoic, an experience the outer path is meant to prepare us for.

Without this non-dual experience and the concurrent transformation it causes in us, experiencing God solely through the path of purification may not even be possible, though it may be possible to become a better person in this way.

True devotion closes the distance between subject and object. We might term this powerful experience of closeness *cleaving*, as in *"Therefore shall a man leave his father and his mother, and shall cleave unto his wife…"*

In order to have the experience of cleaving to God, we must look beneath the appearances of separateness maintained by the ego and see the undivided Wholeness beneath.

This is something the ego can never do: That is not its purpose. It would be like asking our teeth to see, or our ears to taste.

Without the knowledge of looking at the world from the non-dualistic point of view, the search for God would lead only to more and more separateness and more and more despair, as we divided the world into smaller and smaller pieces of exactness and purity, thereby missing the Whole Face of God.

One way to help ourselves is to use language in a new way, a way in which we are not always maintaining the subject/object split, but looking at the words-in-themselves, trying to find what the *Zohar* calls "The Sparkling" within the matrix of the word.

The inner meanings of the word *kavvanah* are one of the ways we can find our way inside the Heart of God.

In order to understand this new approach to *kavvanah*, we want to come out of *memory* and into the present moment, and see what Reality looks like from that point of view.

Coming out of memory, we get to experience the heart of *kavvanah*, which we might call *Pure Presence*, and it is through this gateway that we can enter the throne room of the God Without Form.

Try this:

> *Close your eyes and think about something that is difficult in your life right now. Just imagine it for a few moments. Now: Tune into your body for a moment and notice how it has changed since you began remembering this difficult situation. Probably your pulse has changed, perhaps your breathing, maybe you feel a little tightness—or a lot of tightness!—around your chest.*
>
> *Pick one of these changes, such as your tightness, and just allow it to be there.*
>
> *Drop all of your emotional and remembered associations with it, and simply allow it to be there as pure sensation.*
>
> *What happens?*

If you were able to stay with it, you may even have noticed that this difficult thing, once it was transformed into pure sensation, became something interesting to be with and watch. We might even say it took on a kind of "living quality." It took on a kind of "life of its own" that did not have to do with the sorrow or difficulty it was originally associated with.

In the same way, we can work with the concept of *kavvanah.*

Something is a "thing" if it needs something else— or memory—to define it.

As an example: All truly great art has the quality of seeming to exist as if it were the only thing in the world, without reference to anything else. I don't mean that it does not *refer* to things past, but it exists on its own, with a *timeless, dynamic* and *living* quality.

Kavvanah, in its ordinary definition is what kabbalists would call a *yesh, a thing* or *existence,* and not something that exists in its own right.

In the exercise, when we dropped the emotional connection to the sensations, the problem started to transform into *energy* and no longer needed something to be paired with ("the problem") in order to exist.

Only when it is "the thing in itself" does its true interrelationship with All become apparent.

The Mahayana Buddhists call the thing that exists without reference (or paradoxically, with the complete understanding of the inter-relatedness of all things) "the self-illuminating state of *tathagata*," where *tathagata* means "thus-ness," or "is-ness."

Only when *kavvanah* is something *in itself* can we begin to see the enormous transformative power contained in it, the power to cleave to the Creator.

So *kavvanah* at first seems like it is something to be used *with* something. But if we detach from that and simply see it as its own end, then its true meaning becomes apparent.

We take it out of the realm of "thing" (yesh) and it becomes part of the Shining or Brightness.

Kavvanah is focus, attention and so on. But it turns out that it is not focus or attention *upon some object or action* but the *destroyer of separateness* if we see it for itself.

It then leads directly to *de/vuket*, cleaving to God. It stops being "a thing" and becomes "Itself," with no shadow of a reference point left in the Light of One.

Kavvanah is not something you have to practice *on something else: It is a practice in and of itself.*

It becomes a form of Pure Presence.

In this same way, we can now understand a bit more clearly the type of Will or Desire that belongs to God.

If we simply make God's desire and pleasure over in our own image, we can never understand God's desire to move from the Un-Manifest to the Manifest; from the Un-Created to Created Beings…or His ability to move from the Manifest *back* to the Un-Manifest. If we don't see things as they are, we can never appreciate how the play of the manifest world and the Silence of the Unmanifest support and depend upon each other.

Seen only in the small way, God's Will-Desire can only be a larger version of why we will or want things: to better ourselves in some way, or to give ourselves more pleasure in some way. This reduces God's will-desire to something we already know: The Unknown is left out.

From the limited perspective—which many kabbalists ascribe to—the world is an unfinished place, and only our effort can finish it. This type of thinking leads to ever more separation: It declines to honor the difference God has put in people and their paths, and waits for all things to come under the control of one context. In fact, the world is unfinished, and we *do* need to finish it. But this can occur only as we take on God's attitude and stop looking through the limited eyes of the partial self.

Without this understanding, even if our will is to help others, as long as we see "others" as somehow separate from who we are, our help will be filled with the faint tinge of ego that needs *our* results and recognition for *our* effort. And even more important, this subject/object split will bring the adulteration of the pure, unaffected joy that can be ours when we help non-dualistically, joy we try to eliminate because—paradoxically—it seems egotistical to us. For in Reality, service to God—which is identical with service to others—is a joy-filled thing. As the *Zohar* teaches, "joy is the foundation of the worlds."

What is it like to have Will and Desire without an Object, which is to say without separation between doer and done to? A Desire-Will which engulfs and enhances both partners and melts the distance between God and Man? For from God's point of view there is no separation.

Try this:

> *Close your eyes and imagine for a moment that you are a vessel filled with Light.*
>
> *This Light glows softly within you, and you are filled with it.*
>
> *Stay with this for a few moments.*
>
> *Now, turn your attention to the vessel itself, which in your mind is probably some part of your body, such as its outer and inner walls.*
>
> *Now imagine that this part, too, is Light, not just the interior. Light containing Light.*
>
> *Stay with this.*
>
> *What happens?*
>
> *Now repeat this exercise, only this time let your interior body be filled with desire or will for something. It could be a person, or a particular food, or some material or spiritual goal.*
>
> *Now, in the same way as before, let the container become will-desire as well.*

What happens? Does the goal or desire change? You may find that it becomes more pleasurable in and of itself, and that the urgency you felt associated with the will or desire to accomplish its end is gone, while paradoxically, the will and desire remain.

In a sense, we are being asked to *raise up* our small desires and will, not to something bigger—the way a child thinks about God—but to something completely different, different in the way a shadow is different from the person whose shape it mimics; different as the word "rose" is from the soft-petalled flower that sits on thorny branch in the still summer air.

In Isaiah we read:

Lift up your eyes on high, and behold who has created these things; who brings out their host by number, He calls them all by names by the greatness of His might, and because He is strong in power not one is missing.

Thus the Named God names all things, and Pure-Desire-Without-an-Object is made Manifest-Desire, through which the world is made.

In the same way, the process of *return* is a kind of moving from the many names or things of this world, to the Name which is God and finally to One who is before all Names. In so doing we return the world to *tikkun-healing*, the moment when we see the return of the world and our own bodymindspirits to their Original, undisturbed Wholeness.

> "...*at the time when by His will all things were made, then was His name proclaimed King. And after all things shall cease to be, the Awesome One will reign alone.*"

In this moment in *Adon Olam* we meet God, who has *descended* from the Un-Manifest to become King, a King who will Remain after Creation because His True Nature is not only in the Manifest but in the Un-Manifest as well; a King whose Most Intimate Essence *is, was,* and *will be*.

And He Was And He Is

7   He was, He is, and He shall be in glory.
8   He is One, and there is no other to compare to Him,
9   To consort with Him.
10 Without beginning, without end,
11 Power and dominion belong to Him.

Human beings have two types of intelligence, two faculties through which they can apprehend the world.

The first and most usual is the intelligence created and arbitrated by the ego.

This form of intelligence *compares one thing to another* in order to understand something. It always *stands apart* as the unspoken presence that defines and objectifies the world.

This is *comparative* intelligence and only knows reality by juxtaposing one thing against another.

Comparative intelligence begins existing once the world is named; therefore, it has little to say about the unmanifest and the Silence of God, since these conditions can be apprehended only by entering into a state of no-comparison, the state the great Egyptologist and spiritual thinker Schwaller de Lubicz calls intelligence-of-the-heart.

For with the emergence of the world into being comes the right and the left, male and female, hard and soft, far and near; in short, all the qualities of duality, recapitulating the original splitting of God from the Vacated Space.

When viewed from the vantage point of duality, these qualities are irreconcilable opposites. From the viewpoint of intelligence-of-the-heart, however, both disparate conditions are seen as outpicturings of a third yet higher thing, the new home that reconciles both.

Adon Olam teaches us what the innate qualities of a Creator who was, who is, and who will be, are like.

To understand this statement from intelligence-of-the-heart and not from comparative intelligence, we must understand that this is not a statement that is *within* time or a description of a certain *kind* of time, in this case *eternal time*.

The prayer is not talking about a Being who *lasts forever*. This would limit the Creator to being a *being in time*, just as human beings are in time, *only in this case God's "time" lasts forever!*

Instead, the prayer is describing a Being who is eternal because He is *below time*, as it were; *outside of time; before the* concept *of time even began. Adon Olam* teaches us that God is the *Begetter of Time.*

When we ask *Who?* long enough, and when the ego stops spinning out partial, intellectual, comparative answers, we begin to hear and feel a Silence that is beyond time.

This is not a Witness: The Witness is simply a more neutral, well-behaved sort of ego. Instead, here the witness itself is abandoned in favor of an Invisible Wholeness.

This prayer goes on to talk about power and dominion belonging to God. Again, we must be careful to know *who is listening to these words.* If it is the egoic self, then power has to do with control and its reach. From the egoic point of view then, God is someone who has *total control and total reach.* Hence the word *omnipotent.*

Words like *omnipotent* and *omniscient* are fodder to the ego's fire. We think of them as meaning that *God knows everything and has power over everything in exactly the way "we" would…if we were masters of the universe.* But God is not only the Master of the Known, He is the Master of the *Un-Known,* the *Hiddenness* that lies at the base of each thing.

We might say that God hides *within each thing,* if we only dare to look long enough.

To understand who has this power and dominion, we must first understand Who Is the One who has no one to compare to Him, to consort with Him (*lines eight and nine of the prayer*).

Once the world is made, everything can be compared to everything else, and this—through the medium of comparative intelligence, is the usual way these lines are interpreted: God is the most, and we are small. God is perfect; we are imperfect; God knows All, we know little.

Through this form of understanding, God becomes more and more distant, and we become less and less. And while the ego—always afraid of being killed— sees this as some form of humility (the antidote to its "sin" of existing at all), this is certainly not the kind of relationship a loving Father and Creator seeks to have with his children.

Just as human parents seek to make it possible for their children to grow up and completely fulfill their potential and draw close to the parent in heart and soul, so God wants this for us. From the non-dual point of view, this Desire exists as a Law of the Universe and not as result of reward for something done.

To understand better that portion of the Mind of God we are given to understand then, we must abandon comparative or intellectual understanding and attempt to understand through intelligence-of-the-heart.

The prayer says: "He is one, and there is no other to compare Him to, to consort with Him..."

Here "one" means *One and Not Two*.

This is not a superlative but a statement of fact, a fact that human beings are capable of understanding because it is *essentially where our life springs from: It is our True Nature, and our True Nature is to be Close to God.*

Try this:

> *Imagine for a moment, that the best minds and hearts of humanity have determined, once and for all, that after you die, you are simply and irrevocably dead.*
>
> *There is no Heaven.*
> *There is no Hell.*
> *There are no Angelic Realms.*
> *No after-death dreams, or at least not any that outlast the final destruction of the body.*
>
> *There is no one there to reward you or punish you. Now, you may not realize it, but many—if not most—of our actions come from holding on to this dream.*
>
> *If we were not subtle and learned people, we might act in certain ways so that we would be*

rewarded in heaven with money, or pleasures, or eternal life, and so on.

But because we are subtle, the rewards we are looking for are subtle: We want to know more about the universe, and we believe that after we die we will know more. God will tell us and show us that a connection to the kind of intellect-feeling we have now will continue...only more so.

We believe that the pain we might be in now, whether physical, emotional, or spiritual, will be allayed. Understanding, or some sort of Holding, will happen that will take it away.

And we do good on this earth both in order to avoid punishment and find our way into Heaven.

If you have any doubts that you feel this someplace within yourself, simply go inside and repeat to yourself: "They have really, really, really found that nothing exists after you die."

See how you feel.

Take it as true. It is True.

Now ask yourself: What will I now do with the rest of my life? How will it change my actions, feelings, and thoughts?

Don't say, "It won't," too quickly.

If you find the way in which it does, look closely at the behavior that remains after you eliminate the things you do to achieve an almost invisible sense of safety and meaning.

When you act from what is below that level, the level that does not act from hope or fear, you have a chance of entering into an experience of what "One and Not Two," means.

If you simply go to the depths of this exercise and remain there, you will experience a freedom of being and action you have not often felt; it feels like a singularity or essential core of being that brings you *closer* to God and other human beings rather than farther away.

This Being—and the piece of God that is in you— the One who is *truly eternal,* with no beginning and without end because He is the Antecedent of Time, the Ancient of Days—is the One to whom all power and dominion belong.

This is our God and the only one who we can truly entrust with our souls; that part of our beings beyond our waking or sleeping, pleasurable or painful experiences or even our life and death.

This is the God who was the same before the world was created and the same since the world was created, the Unchanging One who is responsible for all change and for Whom categories do not exist.

This is the One who we can approach only when we are without thought. We must be *bound to Him in heart, body, and soul.*

I Shall Not Fear

12   **He is my God and my ever-living Redeemer,**
13   **The strength of my lot in time of distress.**
14   **He is my banner and my refuge,**
15   **My portion on the day I call.**
16   **Into His hand I entrust my spirit,**
      when I sleep and when I wake.
17   **And with my soul, my body too, the Lord is**
      with me,
18   **I shall not fear.**

It is our lot in life to be afraid. To have no fear in life is to be, on some essential level, psychotic, out of reality.

We come from Beyond Thought and leave for a Place Beyond Thinking. How can we not reasonably be afraid, becoming a *non-thing* after so many years of learning to be "a person"?

And yet the prayer says "And with my soul, my body too, the Lord is with me, I shall not fear."

Fear dies the moment the small and frightened "I" is transformed into the I of God. This does not mean we *are* God—another egoic attempt to pave the way to eternal, egoic bliss. It simply means we are like God's little finger, a portion of the Master of Hiddenness in manifest form. It also means that our identification with the body—the identity the ego holds dearly— has been weakened: We see we are the body—but only to the extent that the body is an outpicturing of something even Greater.

The Lord is with us because without God we are a collection of chemicals, with no association, no growth, no holding together, no life and no death.

But by the Master of Hiddenness we are blown into the Manifest World like warm breath blown into winter air and we become subject to birth and death: We exist for a while and we are gone. Until the next breathing.

The same air is brought back into the Body of God, and God creates again, the Eternal No-Thought, Beyond-Time-One who cannot be compared to anything because He is truly Singular.

It is in our taste of this Singleness, which is within our capacity to experience, that human fear is given a context, and we become willing to be breathed by God.

God is that One who never leaves us and is always Present, closer than air can ever be, breathing for us as we breath for Him.

Finally

We do not pray to make the world Holy.
We pray because the world *is* Holy.

THE CONFIGURATIONS

A Nondual Look into the Partzufim

JASON SHULMAN

What are the Partzufim?

The *Partzufim*, also known in English as Countenances, Faces, Person and Configurations, are arrangements of various combinations of the sephirot in the Tree of Life. Although built on earlier material from the Zohar and from Moses ben Jacob Cordovero, the *Partzufim* as we know them today are the insight of Isaac Luria, the great Kabbalist of Safed, who included but also radically modified Cordovero's systemization when he arrived in Safed just after Cordovero's death.

Essentially, the *Partzufim* are personas, personalities, divine representations, if you will, in the upright configurations of humankind, meaning that they embody human metaphors. One of the great contributions of the partzufic paradigm is that while in earlier models, the sephirot emanated one from the other and had little interaction between each other, these divine personas allow for dynamic interactions that have movement or relationship between God and God's creation.

This allows ongoing creation as a palpable, dynamic presence in the world. The *Partzufim* help solve the eternal problem (which arises specifically in dualistic or theistic systems such as Judaism), wherein one must bridge the distance between an unalterable, unchangeable God and God's creations, between the will of heaven and life on earth.

The *Partzufim* assist, or make possible, the rectification of this world and move the world from chaos to healing. They essentially integrate a holographic principle, a two-way street, in the relationship between the Divine and the Created, in which every bit of creation is filled with the Divine Presence. Thus God and God's creations are shown to be a single thing. The specific *Partzufim* are described later in this monograph.

1. If the *Partzufim* were only an abstract concept, a conceptual trope that might help us, for example, to understand elevated philosophical ideas, then their importance would be limited. But the *Partzufim* can be viewed as *arrangements of reality,* and as such are operating holographically *throughout* reality and not limited to certain realms. When deeply understood, it is the *Partzufim* that unite heaven and earth, the unitive world and this dualistic one, and present to us the potential of consciously living a human life that reflects this union as the natural consequence of being alive.

2. To start, then, let's look at the universe from a physical point of view.

3. Scientists now know that things happen on every level of creation. In other words, there is activity everyplace we look for it, whether that place is big—like the universe—or small, like the sub-atomic world. There is no level of reality where activity—which is to say interaction—is not taking place. Even so-called "empty space" is filled with fluctuations, which constantly bring virtual particles into and out of existence. In other words, even the vacuum of space is boiling with activity.

4. So, we have atoms, and even deeper, the structures of atoms, the vast array of sub-atomic particles and, further, the possibilities of seeing even more deeply into the structures of timespace itself: strings, multi-universes and so on.

5. On the molecular level, we have organic and inorganic chemical interactions. Certain atoms seem to like each other and get together to form molecules, and those molecules interact with each other and form compounds, and compounds, materials... and so on.

6. Our world is built on the basis of these interactions. Interaction is built into the *foundation* of the world. We could say that *interaction is the world.*

7. In this way, the *expression* of the world and the world itself are identical.

8. We might even say—from a philosophical point of view—that this level of interaction is the world's *meaning.*

9. Everything is interacting. Creation, from this point of view, never started and

cannot end. It is an ongoing expression of something deeper. Creation is identical to this interactional relationship.

10. We have explored this idea by learning about the interactions of the sephirot in the Tree of Life.

11. Here we have "qualities" (the sephirot) that interact and that, through the lens of Nondual Kabbalistic Healing, we have turned into a healing modality that involves the changing relationships between the healer and client, and the client's problem as well.

12. But there remains a question that is at the bottom of all of this interacting, a question of how the universe's *motivation* to interact is embodied. In other words, *what* is the vehicle these forces use that causes them to interact?

13. What level of creation is it that "wants" certain chemicals to be attracted to other chemicals? Why do certain sub-atomic structures form from strings? What sets the stage for all this interaction? And so on.

14. These may seem like imponderables but we can make certain progress.

15. In creating the idea of the *Partzufim*, Isaac Luria was revealing the dynamic, creative force that is the mode through which the universe thrives and develops.

16. We could say that the *Partzufim* are the agencies of development, of movement, attraction and repulsion. In other words, they are the underlying "themes" that make inanimate things animate, that are the motive forces behind the curtain of the manifest world.

17. And because they use the metaphor of "family relationships," they are—as we have talked about in our version of these *partzufic personalities*—nondual in the sense that one needs the other to actually have an identity. Thus, to be called "father" you need to have a daughter or son. Kabbalistically speaking, Z'er Anpin, a male partzuf, needs Nukva, the female, to be complete. We could go further and say "male" does not exist except for the existence of "female." If there was no female, we could not say male. One

depends upon the other for its identity. In other words, both individual identities are dependently co-arising and are actually both a single thing *and* two separate things in the same moment.

18. As I have said from the beginning, Kabbalah teaches us that *relationship* is the fundamental theme of this universe and that the *Partzufim* embody this intertwined, networked relationship.

19. *Partzufim*—countenances, faces, personae, configurations—are the human, familial metaphors for these "individuals" (or arrangements) who combine, move apart, and move together again, so that relationship, the interactivity of the universe, can be manifest.

20. *Going further we can say that the Partzufim are the "holders" of this power or perhaps more precisely, "tendency," the tendency and desire to interact.*

21. We must note in addition, that though these metaphors seem anthropomorphic, that is, ascribing human characteristics—like family relationships and tendencies—

to something that is not human, like God, or animals or objects or, in this case, the *Partzufim*, this mode of expression actually points to a deeper and wider insight. It is this: our so-called "human qualities" such as emotion, thinking and so on, are not only *not* exclusive to human beings, but derive automatically from the interactions of fundamental forces and agencies that we are now calling "the *Partzufim*."

22. From this point of view, we no longer have to separate "human" from "nature" since both are made in the same mode. They can now be seen as a single thing since these seemingly anthro(human)po-morphic (in the shape of) qualities are holographically spread through space and time, manifesting in us in a *personal* way and in other creations in other tonalities and resonances, all around the same central idea or relationship.

23. We could also say that the *Partzufim* are the idea of "who" in the universe. This is a subtle idea: "the who" is not a question, as in "who is it?" but a statement of the appearance of a certain fact or level of creation.

24. With the insight into the *partzufic* level, we now have the appearance of "the who," or, to put it a little more correctly, "the who" as a level of reality is invented/ described/revealed through these *partzufic* individuals.

25. So the *Partzufim* are not a human construct we project backwards onto the concept of God, personifying it in this way, but a "lifting up" of a fundamental condition inherent in the depths of creation. We raise it up into our world so we can see the action and effects of the Totality in our everyday lives.

26. Going further, this "who" is not restricted to self-aware beings such as humans (or even self-aware aliens!) but is a feature of every manifest object.

27. Let's put it this way: This entire universe is a "who." There is nothing in this universe that is not a "who." Therefore, we can say that the *Partzufim* is another way of talking about the initial or prior *who-ness* of the universe, the pattern every created thing will follow in its manifestation.

28. This leads us back to the universe's basic theme of relationship—which of course is a description of what happens between two individuals, two separate things, two "who-is-es."

29. *Everything in the entire universe is a "person" of one sort or another.*

30. And while we like to think that we are at the top of the heap, lest we be blinded by our egocentricity, we must remember that rocks feel, that mountains move, that hydrogen has its own form of thought and feeling, that galaxies are not the offspring of content-less forces but are expressions of a different sort of individuality.

31. Life, like the activity I mentioned at the beginning of this essay, is not restricted to one level of creation or another: it is found everywhere there is a "where."

32. Although Luria did not put it this way, we could say that in looking at the *Partzufim*, we are approaching the mystery of why the universe creates "persons," and what the inner reason for the existence of "persons" is. Activity. Relationship. Interactivity.

33. Personhood created the universe, so to speak!

34. And while the traditional emphasis has been on how the *Partzufim* bridge the gap between an unchanging, timeless, absolute (God) and the changing, temporal world, here we have no such problem since we realize that God—who contains all things, all possibilities, all multiplicities, all times and spaces—easily contains the origins of personhood and location, even as it contains impersonal, unchanging-ness, so to speak, the stillness of the absolute.

35. In other words, God and God's creation co-arise as well, need each other and are each other *when they are taken together as an inseparable, co-arising pair. God and God's creation are a single thing.*

36. This *personal-who-level* is holographically spread through every layer and dimension of the universe since it is part of the origin as everything that unfolds is part of the origin. The *Partzufim* are the *basic location* of this personal quality and exemplify this universal movement toward the personal as the unit of creation in our universe.

37. We need to be careful here and not separate "the universe" from "the personal," as if there were a universe that was "filled" by this quality called "the personal." No. As I mentioned before, the universe and the personal are co-arising phenomena. One *cannot* exist without the other.

38. Relationship is all about "who" (the unit of relational interactivity) and the *Partzufim* are the theme of this "who."

39. They are the "directors" or "location" of all that is, the fundamental captains of the universe's industry.

40. Going just a bit further, the *Partzufim* exemplify both the individual (which is something *located*) and the non-locatable pattern that allows individuals to arise in the first place.

41. This means these nondual configurations are both "everywhere" and "somewhere" in the same moment. Unity and duality together forever.

42. It is this remarkable power to create identity that occupies us in this essay, however, since it is that function that is often overlooked as perhaps the most beautiful and holy of creations.

43. Question: Why is this important for us to understand?

44. Answer: Because the *Partzufim* are interacting—or at play—all of the time, in every direction and in every situation we are involved in.

45. Stop for a moment and think about this. You are crossing a street. There are cars and people at the stop light. There are buildings and the sky above them. There are clouds and sunlight and a light breeze blowing. You are wearing a coat imagined by someone, sewn by someone, delivered and sold by someone and it is now on your body. All of these are "who-s," alive centers of consciousness, interrelating each in their own way, either actively or passively. What happens to your own consciousness if you walk across the street with all of this knowledge?

46. We could say that since the *Partzufim* are in fact the very substratum of existence, they are responsible for everything that nature manufactures…including your own brain with its myriad cells, activities and relationships.

47. We know, as an example, that *each cell of your body* contains a mechanism for keeping track of time in the form of a circadian clock located in each cell. Since each cell is in a different space, we have a body that is constantly organizing itself in both time and space in a highly nuanced way.

48. (My research—not the province of this particular monograph—has shown me that self-awareness arises from the minute differences in timing between different sections of the brain and that timings that are too close together or too far apart have consequences for the way in which we experience the world.)

49. Put another way, *all of the partzufic* pattern-making engines are working within you and on you all of the time and there is no situation you go into in

which these "faces," "personas," "captains of organization," are not working at full capacity, since your very brain and its sensory partners *were made by these partzufic perspectives.*

50. Which is to say that the *Partzufim are the local focal points of the universe's fully integrated "desire" or "will" to make "persons" or specific areas of manifestation.* You. Me. Galaxies. Worms and termites....

51. We do not walk into any situation without these *partzufic* parts operating within us. We cannot, since we are *partzufic beings interacting globally and locally in the same moment.*

52. But the nonduality of this goes even further.

53. The *Partzufim* not only function as filters in the sense that we only see what they will let us see, but they additionally function as *creators*, actively *seeking* and *being* signs that the plenum forms itself around and in that way, creating environment and a narrative through which individuals can communicate and relate.

54. The pearl, the grit, and the oyster arise together to make the sparkle.

55. We could say that the *Partzufim* are both the *continuity* and the *densities* and their constant co-arising-s. We see what is there and create what is there.

56. So *Partzufim* are "points of view," both happening and waiting to happen; points of view both *seen* and *created* at the same time.

57. As I mentioned before, the *personality's* purpose is that it is the primary unit of interaction in the universe. In this way, it is not only the most highly organized level of reality (for example: human beings) but the simplest and the most fundamental, the ground of being itself from which all arises.

58. And rather than thinking of the Kabbalistic universe of Atzilut as that level of reality in which the self is non-existent, buried in God, so to speak, so that there is no individuality at all, we could say that Atzilut is that place of the fullest expression of the interrelated-ness of all

---

[1] *Continuity/density* is the way I talk about this co-arising of the absolute and the specific in the discipline of Nondual Shamanism. Please check with The Foundation for Nonduality (www.nonduality.us.com) to find my book about this approach to healing and knowledge of reality.

things, the co-arising of God and God's creations, the inseparability of a one-ness that contains multitudes.

59. Here are the names of the six *Partzufim:*

SEPHIROT	MAIN PARTZUF	DESCRIPTION
Keter	Atik Yomin	Atik Yomin is found in the up-per—or inner—part of Keter. Known as the Ancient of Days and Godly-Delight. It is at the level of absolute oneness with God.
	Arich Anpin	Arich Anpin is known as the Long Face, Slow to Anger, and has the attribute of infinite patience. It is the configuration of the lower part of Keter.
Chochmah	Abba	Father
Binah	Imma	Mother
The Seven Traits or Attributes: Gevurah, Chesed, Tiferet, Netzach, Hod, Yesod and Malchut.	Z'er Anpin	Z'er Anpin—found collectively in the array of the sephirot of Gevurah, Chesed, Tiferet, Netzach, Hod and Yesod—is also known as the Short Face or the Urgent One. Z'er Anpin seeks to unite with Nukva, the "female of Z'er Anpin."
Malchut	Nukva: The Feminine	Malchut and its partzuf, Nukva, are included as part of the Seven Traits (called *Middot* in Hebrew). Nukva is the sister of Z'er Anpin as well as his bride.

---

[2] Atzilut is one of the Four Universes, considered in traditional Kabbalah as the "highest," the one closest to Keter and therefore, to God. It is often translated as the "World of Emanation" or the "World of Causes."

60. Now, let's go further by realizing that *all created things are individuals, which have various levels of awareness or consciousness.*

61. But it would a mistake to think that there are two things: a *partzuf* which is then "filled" with a certain personality...or type of relational interaction.

62. That would be like saying that the element gold is "filled with the color yellow." Instead, it would be more accurate to say that yellow and gold are co-dependently arising. They cannot be separated. The same with waves and ocean, or vibration and atoms or breathing and life...and so on. Form and content are a single thing. *Form* and *action* are the *content* and are all a single thing.

63. While some paths like to think that our body is a temporary illusion and that our soul is something that has been added to this body, that they are two separate things and that the soul even lives on after the body is gone, this new vision would imply that soul and body are a single thing, that the human body is the soul and not the vehicle for something embedded in that physical form.

64. This would mean that the physical is the complete abode of the holy and is the astounding location where divinity's desire (or: *action*) to *be* is manifested.

65. Further, it would mean that the action of eternity is the plenum's continuing creativity, its continual mode of creation— rather than the fact that one particular *personality or person*, in the way in which we understand that, goes on and on.

66. More important, I think, this would also mean that the "desire to connect" would not be something that was added to this physical world or to individual entities as if we were adding water to a glass, but something that was the *same* as the entities themselves. Again: content/action/form all the same co-arising things.

67. In other words: the desire to connect, to be in relationship, co-arises with the physical. It is *identical to the physical*.

68. In a way, this is obvious because to even have something manifest means that the desire to connect is already activated in that object or being. *Connection* means *matter*:

Matter *means* connection. No separation is possible.

69. An example: Arich Anpin, the "long face" or "long suffering," adds a dimension or reveals a dimension to humankind.

70. Arich Anpin and Atik Yomin both come from Keter. Atik Yomin could be called the mitigating *partzuf* that sees Delight in all things. It needs, however, the theme of Will (Arich Anpin) to allow this theme to permeate creation.

71. Does "Will" create "Delight" or "Delight" create "Will?" The question is the wrong question since these two things are inseparable and simultaneously co-arising—if we let go of the linear, temporal view.

72. Just as Delight is a primary motivating force, the delight of Atik Yomin is brought throughout all of creation by the "descending quality" of Arich Anpin.

73. Delight would not be delight unless it had continuity or duration throughout every ongoing moment of creation. We could

say that this "throughout-time quality" is provided by Arich Anpin.

74. So again, each depends upon the other for its existence.

75. Only with both Atik Yomin and Arich Anpin do we get the holographic principle of existence.

76. So we could say that each *Partzuf* is a "thread" that is not "contained" in the universe but of which the universe is made. No universe without them.

77. Finally, let's go a bit further if we can!

78. If we go back to looking at the *Partzufim* as individual personalities, a family, if you will, we could then say—much like a family—that the *partzufim* are *entangling* principles.

79. Their purpose, among others, is to entangle one thing with another. We have myriad examples of this in our human life: we are "entangled" with our families; with our parents, with our lovers and partners, with our community…and so on. This

"entangling" is another way of talking
about a specific aspect of *relationship*.

80. If we think about it, we can see that the
    Partzufim entangle the sephirot with each
    other (since they are composed of various
    combinations of the sephirot...) or, put
    another way, they allow these somewhat
    abstract qualities (the sephirot) to become
    actual forces that both cause inter-
    relationships and relate this new level of
    creation as well.

81. Something is only a force when it is in
    relationship to something. Wind with
    nothing to move is not...wind.

82. Relationship itself is an entangling process.

83. When two things become entangled,
    there is time and space between them.
    This would imply that time and space
    are a condition that matter is in and not
    abstract qualities that can exist without the
    existence of matter.

84. For those of you who have experienced
    deep meditative states, the parallel is that
    consciousness itself seems to cease to exist

when there are no thoughts or feelings—
thought and feelings in this case being the
analog for matter in the universe.

85. From this perspective, we could say that
the *partzufim* are the agents of time and
space, the density or "thought" of the
absolute that together make the manifest
universe.

86. When two people become entangled,
which is to say, have a relationship, they
are a universe.

87. When we cross the street, aware of all the
"who-is-es," we change our perception
of the universe and become a center of a
different type of consciousness, one that
has space and time for something new.

88. This is what healing is: the creation of
spaciousness, possibility, openness, which
is to say, time and space for new creation.

89. The *Partzufim are the baseline thought of
the absolute universe (the first density of the
continuity for those of you who have studied
Nondual Shamanism), the "I" of the plenum
that brings with it this wonderful and terrible
manifest world.*

90. To free us up a bit, we can go further and say that we don't have to follow the example of Isaac Luria and call these basic outlines of relationship "faces," or "personas" or "countenances." We could call them "different times," or "different spaces."

91. As I mentioned before, my own research has shown me that different areas of the brain are in slightly different times. In other words, different sections of the brain (which of course are in different spaces anatomically) are in or out of synchronization in specific ways, and that these ways manifest as different types of consciousness, some helpful, others problematical. Further research may show us the temporal aspects of the *Partzufim* more clearly and in that way, allow us to use them to help various problems. I have already developed one healing called "The Healing of Identity," which, though very efficacious, is too intuitive to be passed on with any degree of certainty or accuracy. Hopefully, more research will allow me to re-visualize this healing so it can be shared.

92. Where does this leave us? My answer for now is very simple: we are not alone.

93. Wherever we go, we are and are *accompanied* by, these fundamental agents of individuality and although we take this individuality as something entirely personal, it is really a creation of both the absolute, continuous aspect of the universe and the co-arising specifics of manifestation and thus, cannot be said to be entirely personally owned. It is something shared with all of creation.

94. In this path, we have never denied the individual nor the divine aspect of the human ego. We have sought only to heal it so that it could take its rightful place as the holder of infinite beauty.

95. The universe is filled with companions, agents of Delight and Will, agents of Incompleteness and Desire, Timelessness, Time-filled, Temporary and Eternal. They are filled with every combination we see in human life.

96. We could say that we have projected human life into some system we call

"partzufic" and simply seen ourselves writ large in the heavens.

97. But we could equally, and perhaps more truthfully, say that being *made* of these themes, we are them in physical form and that if we look in every direction in space and time, we are bound to see these themes replicated in non-human situations.

98. Then it becomes clear that the more we open up, the more spacious we become, the more "themes" we will be able to see in the universe and the more ability we will have to put those themes into action, to revel in them, apply them, live them and love them, to share in the ongoing creativity of the universe, or, more exactly, to share in the meaning of the universe *itself*.

99. It is hard job. But it starts with crossing the street and seeing the "being-ness" of everything you see. It is an amazing experience. People-beings, sky-beings, cloud-beings, building and stone-beings, car-beings, irritable sound-beings, wind-beings, a bit of rain-being…and so on, forever.

100. This is how divine Delight reaches us: by an act of Will, of which we are capable.

101. And this is how Will reaches us: by seeing the Delight we can have as we engage with this force with which we are made.

102. And within all of this, there is—without a doubt—suffering as well. Yet even there, the more spaciousness, the more room there is for compassion about our temporary status as citizens of this universe.

103. We are not looking for perfection but to be awake to everything. We live in a milieu of living beings, living beings who suffer and change against a background of unending Delight. If we can bring this awareness to our everyday life, we are changed forever and can help bring about change wherever we find ourselves.

About the Author

Jason Shulman is an American spiritual teacher whose original work springs from his Judaic and Buddhist background. He is the founder of *A Society of Souls: The School for Nondual Healing and Awakening*, based in the United States and the Netherlands. There he teaches the distinctive body of nondual work he has developed to awaken the human spirit: Nondual Healing, Impersonal Movement and the Work of Return. Jason's main concern has been to develop paths of healing the mind, body and spirit based on his own understanding of the difficulties inherent in the human condition. Through his studies and practice, Jason has developed a unique perspective on human consciousness and the nature of existence. His work seeks to translate this perspective into a replicable and clearly-delineated path for other seekers of truth to follow. He has been especially interested in applying personal spiritual work to methods of transforming society at large. To that end, he has created the MAGI Process, a nondual method of working with conflicts between people, institutions and governments. He is the author of numerous monographs and books, and several albums of his work as a singer and songwriter. More about his work can be found at www.societyofsouls.com and www.nonduality.us.com